T0330009

Community as Leadership

NEW HORIZONS IN LEADERSHIP STUDIES

Series Editor: Joanne B. Ciulla, *Professor and Coston Family Chair in Leadership and Ethics, Jepson School of Leadership Studies, University of Richmond, USA*

This important series is designed to make a significant contribution to the development of leadership studies. This field has expanded dramatically in recent years and the series provides an invaluable forum for the publication of high quality works of scholarship and shows the diversity of leadership issues and practices around the world.

The main emphasis of the series is on the development and application of new and original ideas in leadership studies. It pays particular attention to leadership in business, economics and public policy and incorporates the wide range of disciplines which are now part of the field. Global in its approach, it includes some of the best theoretical and empirical work with contributions to fundamental principles, rigorous evaluations of existing concepts and competing theories, historical surveys and future visions.

Titles in the series include:

Community as Leadership

Gareth Edwards

Associate Professor of Leadership Development, University of the West of England, Bristol, UK

NEW HORIZONS IN LEADERSHIP STUDIES

Cheltenham, UK • Northampton, MA, USA

Published by
Edward Elgar Publishing Limited
The Lypiatts
15 Lansdown Road
Cheltenham
Glos GL50 2JA
UK

Edward Elgar Publishing, Inc.
William Pratt House
9 Dewey Court
Northampton
Massachusetts 01060
USA

A catalogue record for this book
is available from the British Library

Library of Congress Control Number: 2014954561

This book is available electronically in the **Elgar**online
Business subject collection
DOI 10.4337/9781781009222

ISBN 978 1 78100 921 5 (cased)
ISBN 978 1 78100 922 2 (eBook)

Typeset by Servis Filmsetting Ltd, Stockport, Cheshire
Printed and bound in Great Britain by T.J. International Ltd, Padstow

This book is dedicated to my Mum, Rita,
for all her support over the years

Contents

Preface

... outside of community, there is no experience.
(Nancy, 1991, p. 21)

The initial idea for this book originates in my long-standing interest in concepts of distributed leadership and was further shaped by an article I wrote for a special issue published in the *International Journal of Management Reviews* in 2011. A second key influence was the work with which a group of researchers and I were involved that culminated in the publication of an edited book called *Worldly Leadership* in 2012. It was these two strands converging about the same time that inspired my emersion in the literature on community. This seemed to be an avenue for further developing notions of leadership especially in the areas of worldliness, culture and leadership, concepts of distributed leadership and sociological processes of leadership. The book was also inspired by my continued fascination with notions of leadership learning and development. I have made a specific point in this book of discussing how linking leadership and community can help us understand leadership learning and development at a deeper, contextual and critical level.

The book is meant for all levels of students and scholars. It does not, however, cover the basics of leadership theory and therefore some students may find a parallel textbook (for example, Schedlitzki and Edwards, 2014) useful in gaining a broader understanding of leadership.

I hope you enjoy the book.

Gareth Edwards
Bristol, UK
29 August 2014

Acknowledgements

First, I would like to thank Professor Joanne Ciulla for giving me the opportunity and confidence to write this book to contribute towards the New Horizons in Leadership Studies series. I would also like to thank my colleagues at the University of the West of England, Dr Doris Schedlitzki, Dr Peter Simpson and Professor Peter Case, and my good friend and colleague, Professor Sharon Turnbull, for their inspiration through the original research project looking at leadership, culture and worldliness. This was the trigger for the interest in community and leadership. I would also like to thank my partner, Dr Doris Schedlitzki, first for her support and second for her valuable comments on previous drafts before submitting to the publisher, Edward Elgar. Finally, I would like to thank Fran O'Sullivan, Victoria Nicols and Benedict Hill at Edward Elgar for their continued support and advice.

Introduction

In the parade of ideas, concepts seldom march alone.
(Joseph Gusfield, 1975, p. 1)

Wherever one looks within the field of leadership studies, whether as a student or a scholar, you cannot ignore the numerous calls for the inclusion of a better appreciation of context (for example, Jepson, 2009; Osborn and Marion, 2009; Osborn et al., 2002; Porter and McLaughlin, 2006). However, the number of real in-depth considerations of leadership in context that are available in the literature remains limited. This book infers that taking a community perspective on leadership will help to develop a contextually driven focus on the subject. I have previously started a conversation around the idea of community in developing ideas about distributed leadership (Edwards, 2011) and worldly leadership (Edwards, 2012). Working within these areas, it becomes very apparent that leadership is discussed, theorized and researched largely from a Westernized and individualized perspective. Herein, I reflect on papers such as Knights and O'Leary's (2006) consideration of ethical leadership, where leadership theory is criticized for being too focused upon the individual. Similarly, Bolden and Gosling (2006), propose that the literature on leadership and, in particular, on leadership development is based too much on competencies that pushes towards individualistic interpretations of leadership. In response, they argue that a more relational perspective is needed. During the development of this book the notion of relational leadership consistently emerges as a core theme. To this end the book reiterates those that have developed theory and empirical reflections within this field (for example, Cunliffe and Eriksen, 2011; Uhl-Bien, 2006).

Yet, a propensity towards focusing on the individual leader and the dominance of Western ideas on leadership are issues that still pervade the leadership literature. It is in response to these issues that I have attempted to develop themes on leadership from a community perspective. This book therefore is not concerned

1

necessarily with 'community leadership' in the sense of leading community projects *per se*, but concerned more with how theories and frameworks for understanding community can help develop our understanding of leadership. Indeed, as you might expect, the community literature picks up on the march of individualism powered by industrial capitalism and cited by numerous writers since the mid-nineteenth century including Karl Marx (for example, Marx and Engels, 1848), Henry Maine (for example, Maine, 1871), Herbert Spencer (for example, Spencer 1858) and Emile Durkheim (for example, Durkheim 1897), among others, eventually settling with Ferdinand Tönnies's (1887) dichotomy of *Gemeinschaft* [community] and *Gesellschaft* [society] (Gusfield, 1975). From Tönnies's perspective, society differs from community by way of deliberately formed associations for the achievement of mutual goals, such as corporations, political parties and economic contracts (society) and those naturally developing that have intrinsic and non-logical values, such as friendship, neighbourhood and kinship (community) (Gusfield, 1975). These notions have created a society-community dualism in the literature (Gusfield, 1975; Kanter, 1972). It is the contention of this book that ideas of leadership, since the early twentieth century, have been for too long bounded by ideas of *Gesellschaft* and that we need to reflect back upon constructions of leadership based on *Gemeinschaft*. In leadership terms, we have been obsessed with individualized authority leaving little space for a more emergent social phenomenon.

In addition, the literature on leadership appears too obsessed with 'assuming leadership' (using managerial and political positions in organizations and society as a proxy for leadership) (Ahonen et al., 2012) and not enough focused on exploring how leadership is constructed through social engagement. Although the tide seems to be turning with regards to the development of social constructionist perspectives on leadership (for example, Grint, 2005a; Grint and Jackson, 2010), it is the purpose of this book to provide a complementary perspective to ideas of social construction based on a review of the community literature.

Also, through this book, I hope to provide suggestions for researching leadership in more anthropological and cultural terms (for example, Edwards, forthcoming) that will enable latent ideals and lost voices of leadership, which are less defined by Westernized thought, theory and empiricism, to be discovered or rediscovered. To do this, the book reflects on the work of thinkers, philosophers and academics such as Michael Taylor (1982), John MacMurray (1996), Joseph Gusfield (1975), Herbert Gans (1988), Paul Lichterman (1996), Alasdair MacIntyre (1984 [1991]), Robert French (2007, 2008), Amitai Etzioni (1993), Ray Phal (2000), Anthony Cohen (1985), Emile Durkheim (1897 [1951], 1964), Jürgen Habermas (1984), Clifford Geertz (1975, 1983), Victor Turner (1967, 1969), Albert Van Gennep (1908 [1960]), Max Weber (1948), Jacques Derrida (1988, 1997), Michel Maffesoli (1996), Scott Lash (1994), Giorgio Agamben (1993), Benedict Anderson (1983 [2006]), Greg Urban (1996), Jean-Luc Nancy (1991), Maurice Blanchot (1988), William Corlett (1989) and Zygmunt Bauman (2001).

From these reflections, ideas of how leadership can be conceptualized from a community perspective are developed. Some pieces of literature are drawn on in numerous areas in this book, such as Gusfield's work, while other writers, such as Lichterman, attract specific reference in certain areas of the book only – in Lichterman's case around areas of individualism and community. I have also discovered that while some pieces of literature promote ideas of communitarianism (for example, Etzioni, 1993), others are more sceptical and critical and therefore provide a more balanced viewpoint of community (for example, Gusfield, 1975). Hopefully I equally provide a balanced view that uncovers the inherently critical aspects of taking a community view of leadership.

In the remainder of this introduction I shall explore in greater depth the purpose of this book based on a response, as proposed above, to criticisms regarding the individualized and Westernized focus of leadership studies and research. This response particularly draws on the two perspectives of leadership that have inspired the focus of this book – distributed leadership and worldliness. I shall start by summarizing these themes and explaining the link to community.

DISTRIBUTED LEADERSHIP: MOVING AWAY FROM INDIVIDUALISM

'Leadership' is a concept we often resist. It seems immodest even self-aggrandising, to think of ourselves as leaders. But if it is true that we are made for community, then leadership is everyone's vocation, and it can be an evasion to insist that it is not. When we live in the close-knit

ecosystem called community, everyone follows and everyone leads.
(Palmer, 2000, p. 74)

I saw this quote recently when attending a conference keynote presentation by Professor Susan Madsen of Utah Valley University in the US. The quote intrigued me as it seemed to reflect some level of focus for this book. It mentions the importance of community when discussing leadership. It also mentions a critical resistance of the subject of leadership, which interests me as a leadership scholar. And last, it infers distributed leadership as an integral notion linked to ideas and the enactment of community. Within this last sentence, however, there is the inherent problem that my students often level at me when discussing distributed leadership – if everyone is leading, who is following? I remind them at this stage, as the quote alludes to above, that we must see distributed leadership in a fluid frame and from that sense everyone may be leading, but not necessarily at the same time nor for the same reasons. Similarly, everyone is following, but not necessarily at the same time nor for the same reasons. This, I believe, gives a good account of how distributed leadership may be conceptualized and enacted in a community setting.

Distributed leadership, as a concept, has had a high regard recently in the contemporary literature, with key contributions particularly by Peter Gronn (2002, 2008, 2009a, 2009b), Alma Harris (2004, 2008, 2009a, 2009b) and James Spillane (2006). Some earlier work on leadership as process by Diane Marie Hosking (1988, 2007) also contributes to this field. Reviews of the distributed field can be found in a recent journal special issue (see Bolden, 2011; Thorpe et al., 2011) and I will not replicate these here, but instead provide brief discussions of key aspects of the distributed approach.

Gronn (2009b), for instance, describes the idea of distributed leadership as a rallying point for those commentators searching for 'post heroic' leadership alternatives. While Gronn's work underscored a refocus on the topic of distributed leadership, the concept is not new and stems from writings by Benne and Sheats (1948) and Gibb (1954). Other recent publications (Edwards, forthcoming; Sveiby, 2011) also point to evidence of concepts akin to distributed leadership going back further into indigenous community history. What we are witnessing in modern times may be better described as a renaissance of the idea of distributed or collective leadership in current Western societies. Having said this, though, further developments in this area could be initiated in at least two ways. These avenues of development are lined by the need for a wider recognition of distributed leadership from a contextually driven way across differing organizations (Currie et al., 2009; Gosling et al., 2009; Gronn, 2009a; Spillane and Diamond, 2007). For example, the mainstay of the literature regarding distributed leadership appears to have a heavy emphasis on the education sector (for example, Currie et al., 2009; Gosling et al., 2009; Harris, 2008, 2009a; Leithwood et al., 2009; Spillane, 2006; Thurston and Clift, 1996). The relevance to other forms of organization, especially in the private sector, therefore remains a contested area and up for discussion and empirical investigation. There is a need therefore to understand how leadership might be distributed across differing forms of organization, based on structure and context. Discussion of the literature around community, I hope, will help develop themes along these lines.

Second, recent discussions regarding distributed leadership have intimated towards the concept being based on notions of emergent leadership. For instance, Bolden and colleagues (2008, p. 11) have commented that the collective approach to leadership 'argues for a less formalized model of leadership where leadership responsibility is dissociated from the organizational hierarchy. It is proposed that individuals at all levels in the organization and in all roles can exert leadership influence over their colleagues and thus influence the overall direction of the organization.' However, in a later paper by the same authors (Gosling et al., 2009), they suggest that there is a need to recognize social, political and power relations within organizations when discussing and researching distributed or collective leadership. This implies that there is a need to understand distributed leadership from within organizational context and culture. Indeed, Spillane and Diamond (2007) advise that distributed leadership is a function between leaders, followers and their situation, they go on to recommend that this is heavily influenced by organizational structure and setting. Exploration outside the context of the education sector and within differing organizational settings therefore is paramount. However, as this book explores, this could be further elaborated at the societal level by exploring notions of community. Linking distributed leadership to societal context resonates with a second area of the literature that seems relevant here: worldliness and leadership.

WORLDLY LEADERSHIP: MOVING AWAY FROM WESTERN THINKING

The worldly concept builds on the literature concerning the 'worldly mindset' and 'worldliness' (Mintzberg, 2004; Mintzberg and Gosling, 2003). 'Worldliness' according to Mintzberg (2004) is quite different to the idea of globalization in that it involves taking a closer look as opposed to a distant look at the world. Turnbull (2009) advocates an alternative view to 'global leadership' is needed owing to four limitations that have been identified, (1) global leadership is often shorthand for Western managers overseas; (2) defining a set of universal traits for leadership is impossible; (3) leadership is contextually driven; and (4) leadership can be seen as a dynamic social process (Turnbull, 2009). The worldly leadership concept addresses these shortcomings and has been defined as 'seeing all kinds of different worlds (often worlds within worlds) from close up and taking action . . .' (Turnbull, 2009, p. 91). From this literature there has been a push to develop an understanding of leadership in indigenous cultures (Turnbull et al., 2012). This book contends that this push towards studying leadership in indigenous cultures has been without an exploration of the knowledge that may already exist from understanding how communities work and how they can be conceptualized (see Edwards, forthcoming). While this book is not directly in the vein of ideas of leadership and worldliness, it does provide some basis for developing research and thinking in the area through a better understanding of how one might interact with communities and hence of leadership constructed in differing social settings.

WHAT IS COMMUNITY?

While the book will draw out the extensive and varied responses to this question in the main part of the book, it is important to note here some of the reflections from the literature that push towards a generic understanding of the concept. For instance, Michael Taylor suggests that community is a 'horribly open-textured concept' (1982, p. 2) going on to describe the many ways the term is used from communities in villages, towns and cities to monastic and utopian communities and intentional communities through to ideas such as the 'academic community' or the 'business community'. Owing to this variety of uses for the concept it is difficult to imagine an overall definition of the concept, something we hear over and again in the leadership literature. Taylor, however, does make reference to some core characteristics in communities: (1) common beliefs and values; (2) relations between members should be direct and many-sided; and (3) reciprocity, in the sense of mutual aid, cooperation and sharing. Taylor also describes links between community and fraternity, friendship and sense of belonging (concepts discussed in more detail later in the book). He also puts forward the notion that liberty is only possible in community. While Taylor's work sets out quite neatly the idea of community, one may contest his conclusions for being too idealistic and that communities may be made up of people, for instance, with slightly differing beliefs and values.

Another author who encapsulates ideas of community is John MacMurray (1996), whose comments on community give some level of introduction to the concept. MacMurray appears adamant that community is the normal state for human beings and that we can only be human in community and community constitutes individual personality. Still, MacMurray suggests that community cannot be brought about by organization as it is not functional but organic. He defines community as a group of individuals united in common life and acting together in communion – a unity of persons as persons. He points out, with regard to this last point, that community assumes individuals are independent and self-contained with the sharing of one's life a matter of personal choice. Community, he goes on to say, is constituted and maintained by mutual affection, not formalized functions. The structure of community is the 'network of the active relations of friendship between all possible pairs of its members' (1996, p. 166).

While these comments give the reader an introduction to the concept they also exemplify some of the critical issues presented back to the reader later in this book, one critical issue being the positivity of the concept of community – that it is inherently a good thing. This is a perspective we might need to challenge given the level of exclusivity that communities can create. Although MacMurray (1996, pp. 167–8) does touch on this in his writing around the time of the Second World War, the positive discourse associated with community is pervasive and this will be challenged at stages in this book. But at this stage and in light of the discussion provided earlier in this introduction, it is important to stress the similarity of these issues with community and the concept of leadership, in the sense that leadership has been argued to be romanticized (Meindl, 1995; Meindl et al., 1985) and is seen as an inherently positive concept (Collinson, 2012). This connectivity is the central spine of this book and it is hoped that by exploring this central spine, the book may provide impetus for future exploration of concepts relating to community in the field of leadership studies.

A GENERAL OVERVIEW OF THE BOOK

When reading through the literature on the subject of community it becomes quite clear that there are similarities in the issues, problems and perspectives to those highlighted in the leadership literature. For example, in Joseph Gusfield's (1975) concise discussion on community he accentuates, in the introduction, the ambiguity of the concept of community and its exclusive split in terms of being geographical (using geographical locations to study community – for example, urban, village, neighbourhood and so on) and relational (the quality or character of human relationships). Ambiguity has been an ongoing issue in the leadership field, where scholars for decades have been waxing lyrical with regards to the non-definition of the term (for example, Bass and Stogdill, 1990; Burns, 1978). Empathy can be held with Gusfield's view on definition of community in respect to leadership and community, or leadership as community, in that he does not offer a definition, as to do so would limit the value to students and readers, because, as Gusfield (1975, p. xvii) states:

> . . . concepts are best understood by seeing how they are used, by examining their historical developments, by showing their contrasting concepts and even by criticizing their claims and uses.

It is hoped that this book will provide some basis for understanding the use of the concept leadership in modern society while examining historical developments and even criticizing various claims about leadership found in contemporary society. This will be done through an exploration of perspectives of community.

The book therefore looks at a variety of differing approaches to community and explores what, if anything, these perspectives can provide us with in our understanding of leadership. These perspectives include a fresh look at the link between individualism and leadership in Chapter 1, a reflection on the role of leadership in developing a sense of belonging in Chapter 2, a further look at friendship, social networks and leadership in Chapter 3. In Chapter 4, the book explores the role of symbolism and aesthetics in leadership and Chapter 5 draws on ideas of liminality and social drama to discuss how they may have an impact on leadership and leadership development. Chapter 6 relates to ideas of community as communicative and discusses elements of language and ethics. Chapter 7 takes a slightly more postmodern and critical perspective and looks at issues of discourse, fluidity, finitude, love and death. Last, the concluding chapter highlights the main themes emerging throughout the book and discusses these in light of leadership learning and development and future research agendas.

1. Leadership and individualism

> The West is in the cold season of excessive individualism and yearns for the warmth of community to allow human relations to blossom.
> (Etzioni, 1993, p. x)

As described in the introduction it seems that concepts of leadership shift between individualistic and distributed perspectives that are reflected in the duality of notions of society [*Gesellschaft*] and community [*Gemeinschaft*]. A push towards *Gesellschaft* and ideas of society develops ideas of individualism in leadership studies and a push towards *Gemeinschaft* and concepts of community develops ideas of a distributed nature when discussing leadership. As also pointed out in the introduction there appears to be a propensity in contemporary writing on leadership that errs towards the individual. On the surface, therefore, taking a community perspective on leadership, as this book does, might redress the balance. However, as we shall see in this chapter, the issue of individualism and community is a little more complex. For instance, individualism can be seen as integrated into concepts of community (Delanty, 2003 [2010]) and that what we witness then is a dynamic duality of individualism within and about concepts of community. In Durkheim's (1897 [1951]) work (cited in Gusfield, 1975, p. 15) he suggests that organic solidarity could not be sustained without risk to the individual personality. Also Lichterman (1996) proposes community relies heavily on ideas of individuality. Other writers (for example, Sandal, 1982; Schaar, 1983) have also highlighted that the self is constituted by community (for example, Corlett, 1989; MacMurray, 1996).

Moreover, MacMurray (1996) says that the development of the individual is the development with his or her other. He explains this by underlining that we are part of that from which we distinguish ourselves; hence if we see ourselves as individuals outside larger groups or communities, there is still the relationship with the group by this separation. He draws this out further by using a religious example of solitude where he suggests that the withdrawal into self is an affirmation of personal dependence not an escape from the relationship with the other. While keeping MacMurray's comments in mind, the chapter explores differing conceptualizations of individualism. Dipping into the literature on individualism will help to uncover a level of complexity that does not appear apparent when looking at the leadership literature.

INDIVIDUALISM

> Perhaps people do not make distinctions between leaders and the institutions they lead.
>
> (Gans, 1988, p. 41)

Gans (1988) elaborates on the quote above by suggesting that chief executive officers (CEOs) of organizations and presidents of countries do not achieve organizational successes by themselves, yet they are often given historical immortality as doing so. This is indicative of the individualistic perspectives of leadership that pervade the literature (Grint, 2005b; Jackson and Parry, 2008; Knights and O'Leary, 2005, 2006), where leadership studies concentrate on the behaviour, personality or style of particular individuals deemed to be leaders defined by their role (Balkundi and Kilduff, 2006; Friedrich et al., 2014). Individualism, though, as Gans points out, comes in varying guises. At a basic level, he recommends that it is the pursuit of individual freedom and of personal control over environmental factors, the ability to make decisions in social settings. He also describes it, however, as an ideology, one that seems to have gripped the US culture. From this early point, we might relate the leadership literature's link to individualism as one derived from the American focus that the empirical and conceptual literature has enjoyed for many years (Burns, 2005). Individualism has come to mark modernity and as Scott Lash proposes, the 'We' of modern times 'has become a set of abstract, atomized individuals' (1994, p. 114). In this vein Gans (1988) also advises that individualism of 1980s America was associated with capitalism, and that individualistic values play a larger role during periods of prosperity. But Gans also links individualism to personal development, a link to leadership discussed further below, and warns against confusing individualism based on personal development with selfishness and greed. In this sense, he suggests that individualism is attacked for having a harmful effect on community. These attacks, he says, propose that individualists deprive themselves of many financial and social benefits of community. He goes on to argue, though, that individualism is social, implying that we can only survive as individuals because we are in and of society, as expressed in the opening section to this chapter. He also critiques the over-idealistic perceptions of community put forward by some writers (for example, Bellah, 1985), which suggest a quasi-religious existence. This relational notion of individualism and community is the general focus of this book and needs further exploration in relation to leadership. The focus of the book will also help to identify areas when this can be further elaborated. But first it appears important to refer to the work of Paul Lichterman owing to his views around ideas of personalism and individualism. These ideas enable a broader perspective of individualism and its relation to community to be taken.

PERSONALISM

Early on in Paul Lichterman's (1996) book, *The Search for Political Community*, he makes a distinction between what he calls 'instrumental or utilitarian individualism' and 'personalism'. Instrumental individualism, he indicates, is the easier individualism to identify in society. This is where individuals build affluent lifestyles through careful calculation. What he describes as 'personalism' is more akin to the ways of speaking or acting that highlight a unique, personal self. It is personalism with which Lichterman is concerned when discussing individualism and community and stresses it as seeking self-fulfilment and individualized expression. He proposes that personalism is interested in growth through personal development as opposed to growth through material means. He acknowledges that within personalism there is a supposition that individuality has inherent value and upholds the personal self and that this has been criticized as being overly narcissistic and self-centred. Although personalism has this orientation towards upholding the self and is often in tension with community ideas, Lichterman contends that this is not at the expense of community ideas, but is in relation to community. For example, he describes individuality as not pre-existing culture but being a cultural accomplishment and personalism is developed in a kind of community that emphasizes norms of highly individualized expression.

Lichterman's main thesis therefore is to imply that personalism plays a role in the construction of community ideas and suggests that this could be 'at best' a counterweight to community ideals and 'at worst' a looming threat. He believes previous writers (for example, Bell, 1976; Lasch, 1979; Rieff, 1966) have failed to recognize any positive impact of personalism on aspects of community and instead paint a picture of hedonistic personalism taking over culture. At this juncture it is worth reflecting on whether this is how leadership theory is being portrayed. Leadership theory could be framed as being painted as the hedonistic personalism in a reactionary way due to the lack of cultural and community perspectives. Maybe the discussion needs to critically reflect on this and advocate, as Lichterman does, a counterweight perspective. One could argue, for instance, that the criticism of leadership from an individualistic perspective (for example, Knights and O'Leary, 2006) and indeed perspectives on toxic and bad leadership (Kellerman, 2004; Lipman-Blumen, 2005) 'assume leadership' (Ahonen et al., 2012), in the sense that they label people in positions of power as leaders, whether they are seen by those around them 'as leaders' outside their role or not.

When considering criticism levelled at leadership theory, suggesting that is of an individualized nature, it would appear that while some writers are discussing this in terms of instrumental individualism (for example, Knights and O'Leary, 2005, 2006), others describe it more in terms of narcissistic personalism (for example, Ford et al., 2008). There is further a wealth of leadership development approaches based on ideas of self-development (for example, Edwards et al., 2002), to the extent that leadership development is a proxy for self-development. Additionally there are the increasing ideas of the authentic self as effective leadership (for example, Avolio and Gardner, 2005; Avolio et al., 2004; Bass and Steidlmeier, 1999; Caza and Jackson, 2011; Gardner et al., 2005, 2011; George, 2003; Luthans and Avolio, 2003; Shamir and Eilam, 2005; Walumbwa et al., 2008; Yammarino et al., 2008). All these aspects of leadership are being debated in the literature but are not explicitly addressing ideas such as Lichterman's discussion on personalism (hedonistic, narcissistic or otherwise) and instrumental individuality. From this point, therefore, ideas of and critics of ethical, authentic or toxic or bad leadership may benefit in their conceptual development from making use of the concept of personalism and/or instrumental individuality.

Moreover, this discussion regarding individualism, personalism and community seems to suggest taking a more relational perspective. This is similar to ideas being developed in the leadership literature on a relational perspective (for example, Cunliffe and Eriksen, 2011; Uhl-Bien, 2006). From this perspective leadership is seen as inter-subjective – *'as a way of being-in-relation-to-others'* (Cunliffe and Eriksen, 2011, p. 1430, emphasis added) and recognizes the importance of the relationship (Gergen, 2009) as opposed to the individual only. It seems, then, to take a community perspective on leadership is to take a relational perspective. Yet, what a community perspective appears to be adding in this instance is a deeper sense of the individual in relation to community and hence to ideas of leadership.

If we take this perspective, therefore, we might see ideas of leadership, such as servant leadership (Greenleaf, 1977), as too idealistic, and reflect on the individual in relation to leadership and followership and again then in relation to community. For example, Lichterman (1996) uses the case of volunteering in the community that, on the surface, is seen as an unselfish act, a case of servant leadership maybe, yet he also states that the person volunteering also gets something out of the relationship with the community – a sense of fulfilment. Maybe we should reflect back on those we construct as leaders and not be too surprised that they may get something from the leader-follower relationship too. This would serve to say that some ideas of leadership, such as servant leadership, are too idealistic in the sense that they go too far towards followership and that a relational view might rein this back a little towards understanding what the individual leader or indeed individual follower is getting out of the relationship and how this is moderated by the relationship with the context. Without taking a relational perspective we tend towards the individual leader or follower but without understanding their motives and hence their personalism. As Keith Grint (2010a, p. 22) says:

> . . . leaders are not heroic knights on horseback rescuing damsels in distress, they are instead . . . figures, fighting . . . their own demons.

Although I have taken this slightly out of the context in which Grint discusses leadership, I do see this exemplifying the idea that we tend to reflect too much on and/or construct the leader as the heroic, as Ford et al. (2008) suggest and is core to criticism of individualistic concepts of leadership, levelled by other scholars (for example, Knights and O'Leary, 2006). This very criticism, however, has a tendency to perpetuate an inherent heroic perspective and does not account for or explore a level of personalism in the role of leader to which this criticism is aimed. There is hence a lack of knowledge of these individuals and the extent to which they are, as Grint describes it, 'fighting their own demons'. Without such additional explora-tion, we are in danger of developing characters and caricatures of leaders in society whereby we construct the heroic figure without understanding their personalism.

CHARACTERS AND CARICATURES OF LEADERSHIP

Following on from the discussion above, this section develops a critical theme around ideas of leadership represented as character and caricature. The role of characterization in more general studies of culture and community has been criticized for being an inaccu-rate representation of individuals (Urban, 1996). In Urban's view this is owing to a lack of connection between the sensible (being perceptible by the senses) and the intelligible (having meaning). Characterization, he suggests, breaks the link between perception and knowledge of social interaction. Yet as Agamben (1993, p. 34) points out, 'whatever being always has a potential character', and the process of characterization in this sense could reflect Agamben's idea of being-in-act and implies potentiality. Agamben links this to the ethical (which I discuss in more detail in Chapter 6) whereby he recommends that the only experience of the ethical is the experience of being one's own potentiality and possibility. This appears to reso-nate with notions of leadership that reflect a representation of the leader as ultimately being oneself and developing those about them to know and be themselves (for example, Goffee and Jones, 2000).

The literature has already recognized this issue in relation to leadership and management being disembodied through character (for example, Ropo and Parviainen, 2001; Ropo and Sauer, 2008; Sinclair, 2005). The suggestion is that leadership study is lacking a bodily and sensory connection through experience (Ropo and

Parviainen, 2001). Furthermore, Sinclair (2005) has suggested that there is a lack of appreciation of bodily aspects such as gestures, stature, posture and voice in management education. The suggestion therefore is that a deeper reflection on the process of characterization is worth pursuing in relation to the study of leadership. Through an exploration of leadership as community, themes around the construction of leaders as characters can be uncovered. For instance, the performativity of certain concepts in the leadership domain, such as authentic (for example, Avolio and Gardner, 2005), ethical (for example, Mendonca and Kanungo, 2007), transformational (for example, Bass and Riggio, 2006) and charismatic (for example, Conger and Kanungo, 1987; House, 1977), pressurize not just those aspiring to be leaders (cf. Ford et al., 2008) but also those searching for leaders or being pressurized to search for leaders, to search for a particular character. This is to the extent that we might construct fellow workers as these characters similar to how Alvesson and Spicer (2010) describe metaphors of leaders as saint, sinner, buddy, gardener, commander or cyborg. The suggestion, therefore, is that this characterizing is enhanced through the performativity of such concepts in the literature that also causes society to further disembody leadership and turn it into a caricature.

MacIntyre's (1984 [1991]) work – *After Virtue* – seems to be a good place to start in the exploration of leader as character. For example, MacIntyre (1984 [1991], p. 30) describes the manager as character:

> ... the obliteration of the distinction between manipulative and non-manipulative social relations ... [and is] not able to engage in moral debate.

Drawing on MacIntyre, I argue that the 'character' of leader may suffer the same fate as being popularized within contemporary business literature (see Ford and Harding, 2007 for a critique) may have developed certain characters that are constructed as inherently moral or inherently immoral. These issues thus bring into question the very use of the leadership discourse in business organizations. The argument therefore is that for the concept of leadership to 'fit' organizations, it is developed into a character role format as if written into a play. This procedure consequently disembodies leadership from reality and hence suggests a fate of becoming caricatured. This seems a reasonable proposition given Weber's ideas of 'ideal-type' (Weber, 1949, cited in Gusfield, 1975). Weber's idea of 'ideal-type' is as described by Gusfield as an imagined construct and described by Weber (1949) as:

> . . . not a description of reality but it aims to give unambiguous means of expression to such a description.

Gusfield (1975) explores this with reference to the concepts of 'bureaucracy', 'capitalism' and 'community'. He suggests that ideal-types are 'heuristic tools, helpful in understanding reality but in themselves not a version of real situations' (Gusfield, 1975, p. 13). In this description Gusfield highlights the danger of using ideal-types – reification – in treating an abstract, analytical term as if it were descriptive and empirical. This is what happens when tagging occurs in leadership studies, for example, using an ideal-type to try and describe certain 'forms' of leadership, such as ethical leadership. The outcome of this tagging is a reification of ideas of leadership that then develops into a process that can be described as character-izing and caricaturing. For instance, relating leadership and leaders to metaphors, as do Alvesson and Spicer (2010), promotes a carica-tured viewpoint on leadership by highlighting exaggerated views on leader identities.

Maffesoli (1996) also writes about the idea of 'ideal-type' but he uses the notion of persona or changeable mask. He takes a more dramaturgical sense in his writing, suggesting that the idea of the changeable mask 'blends into a variety of scenes and situations whose only value resides in the fact that they are played out by the many' (Maffesoli, 1996, p. 10). This resonates with leadership as a mask, discussed further in Chapter 4 and paraphrased a little here. The additional idea could also be that leadership is a persona to be played out in differing situations. Interestingly, Maffesoli goes further and proposes that emblematic figures such as saints and heroes act as ideal-types, they are, however, 'empty "forms", matrices in which we may all recognize ourselves and commune with others' (1996, p. 10). Leadership therefore could also be seen as an empty form to which we relate to recognize ourselves and that this is historically driven through the story making of the heroic (Ford et al., 2008).

To develop the idea of 'character' further we might link it to ideas of community, and, particularly, symbolic representation of community. For instance, Gusfield highlights the idea of symbolic construction, which refers to 'a process of creating and signifying the existence and character of persons and objects by the ways in which human beings conceptualize, talk about and define them' (Gusfield, 1975, p. 24). I have briefly discussed ideas of symbolic representation in relation to the leadership literature previously (Edwards, 2011) whereby leadership is represented by symbolism of and from community. I continue this discussion in Chapter 4, but here we can briefly emphasize images of good and bad as metaphors (for example, Alvesson and Spicer, 2010), from religious forms of 'the saint' and 'the sinner' to the dualist notions of 'the good deity' and 'the evil deity', to more contemporary comic book iconography of 'the hero' and 'the villain' (see Edwards et al., forthcoming a). This idea of leadership represented through symbolism appears to resonate with the idea of 'character' in that if one is to take a community perspective, then the character of leadership is represented through the symbolism within the community. As I show in Chapters 4 and 6, ethicality and the representation of leadership are enacted through symbolic community representation. The argument is that this symbolic representation disembodies leadership through the process of abstraction and tends to progress further to become caricature.

Interestingly, scholars have linked leadership to caricature relatively early on. Hollander and Julian (1969, p. 388) made the following observation:

> . . . two research emphases represented by trait and situational approaches afforded a far too glib view of reality. Indeed, in a true sense, neither approach ever represented its own philosophical underpinning very well, and each resulted in a caricature.

Hollander and Julian's paper does not explore this much further and this book seeks to make a contribution here by developing the theme. For example, the continued process from 'character' to 'caricature' of leadership through being tagged is well articulated again by Gusfield in the work of Cobban (1964) concerning the French Revolution. Gusfield highlights Cobban's conclusions regarding the view that the French Revolution was a 'bourgeois' revolution. As Gusfield (1975, p. xx) paraphrases:

> Such views of social structure were not those of the actors of the time. Instead, he asserts they are the ways in which the historians and

sociologists utilize contemporary perceptions and concerns to build a mythical past and affirm their commitment to a particular impact of the French Revolution as a myth which governs the present.

This example enables us to make the link from character to caricature whereby the further away from the 'actors of the time' the further we characterize and then eventually caricature concepts such as leadership in a social setting. For instance, reading Learmonth (2005, p. 620) there is a quote used from the research that reflects this:

> . . . just as a caricature I would make the observation that many administrators in the 70s and 80s the top ones were employed mainly, well mainly, for their brain power per se as I say a lot of them were intellectual Oxbridge graduates and so on.

The notion of leader or leadership as caricature appears to resonate with Agamben's 'dumb silence of the comic body' (1993, p. 47), whereby leadership as an idea is made dumb or silenced through a process of parody.

COSTUME AND LEADERSHIP

To develop notions around character further there are other, more theatrical, references that can be made, such as social drama (discussed later in the book), the stage set in the sense of place and space (also discussed later in the book). An interesting addition to these perspectives, however, is costume. For the development of this theme I draw on Joanne Ciulla's (2013) work on critically reviewing, through historiography, the leadership of Nelson Mandela. First, she highlights that Mandela saw himself as an actor playing various roles, which relates to the ideas of character and caricature discussed above. Ciulla discusses in detail Mandela's life story as the basis for his authentic leadership (for example, Shamir and Eilam, 2005) and particularly elaborates on Mandela's apparent enjoyment in playing various roles, which Ciulla uses to question the concept of authentic leadership. If one is playing a role, to what extent are we able to be genuine or authentic? Of further importance here is Ciulla's (2013) description of Mandela's seeming obsession with his appearance and more specifically with dress. His appearance appears extremely important to him throughout his life:

One oddity about Mandela and biographies of Mandela is the amount of attention Mandela and other writers give to his clothing. For Mandela, dressing well and dressing right for the occasion are important aspects of how he sees and presents himself to the world.

(Ciulla, 2013, p. 166)

Ciulla goes on to describe how this connection to dress was developed through appreciating smart suits worn by a chief with whom he lived and the connection Mandela recognized between dressing like a white man and being equal to one. Ciulla uses biographical evidence to stress the meticulous nature in which Mandela dresses and ensures he is 'dressing the part' in major events in his life. This culminated, as Ciulla describes, in him wearing the shirt of the Springbok rugby team at the 1995 rugby world cup final, an episode that now immortalizes the Rainbow Nation. It looks as if various 'costumes' enabled him to create various characters that included that of lawyer, revolutionary leader, the 'Black Pimpernel', president and grandfather. Herein, therefore, we see evidence of an important link between leader, costume and the creation of character. Ciulla concludes by asking – Who is Nelson Mandela? In response, she states that he was a great symbol and 'an enigmatic person who emerged from prison accustomed to concealing his emotions behind a mask' (Ciulla, 2013, p. 168). These concluding points about Nelson Mandela's concealment of emotion behind a mask seem to resonate with issues of leadership and symbolism in that the mask is a symbolic representation of the leader and reinforces the character through costume.

LEADERSHIP AS ROLE

Last, the reflections on individualism, character and costume also appear to help with the notion of leader as a role or a position. Urban (1996), for example, describes a role as a 'bundle of rights and duties' (p. 118), it seems leadership studies has been searching for the exact bundle of rights and duties for leaders, maybe we are better to think of the rights and duties of numerous roles of leadership in a shifting pattern of social engagement. Additionally, Urban asks the question as to whether individuals act out roles owing to the way they want their lives narrativized or whether they play out these roles according to how they have previously narrativized a future.

This appears to be an interesting perspective for leadership, to what extent do individuals play out roles of 'the leader' based on internal reflection of self or internal reflection on a future self.

Urban also highlights the roles of 'ceremonial fathers' and 'ceremonial mothers'. These are roles played out in certain indigenous communities and are not the real mother and father but representations of those kinship links within a ceremonial space. This begs the question as to whether leaders are seen as roles reminiscent of ceremonial mothers and fathers within the ceremonial space of the organization or social grouping. Urban goes on to feature the work of Sullivan (1988), who talks about the centre of a ceremonial space where individuals gain the most direct contact with the sacred and the divine. This seems to resonate with ideas of leadership generally (Grint, 2010b), but also with ideas of the charismatic (Weber, 1947). Leadership therefore is created as a ceremonial space within organizations where one can meet the sacred and divine and this is transgressed onto expected roles of leaders in organizations, hence furthering the character and caricature process. This also appears to link to a discussion held later in the book around leadership and social drama (see Chapter 5).

SUMMARY

This chapter has explored ideas about individualism, personalism, character, costume and community and it looks as if ideas of leadership appear to be constructed in context from an interplay between ideas of the individual, the culture representation of individualism, personalism and the context. Laurie Lee describes this interplay a little when he describes an outing as a small boy in his book *Cider with Rosie*:

> Everything began to appear comic strange . . . We began to look round fondly at our familiar selves, drawn close by this alien country.
> (Lee, 1959, p. 193)

This quote aptly describes the conclusions one can make from this chapter in the sense of ideas of the 'familiar self' through personalism, towards ideas of relational aspects between each other, in the sense of looking towards others' 'familiar selves' and, last, how all this interacts with the context and culture – 'the bringing closer through alien context' experiencing community and society. Leader-follower relationships, therefore, may be developed through this complex multitude of interactions with the self, others, context and culture. In the remaining chapters we shall take a deeper look at these interactions.

2. Leadership and a sense of belonging

Any attempt to pluck 'community' and personal relations out of specific contexts is an exercise fraught with difficulties and pitfalls.

(Phal, 2000, p. 60)

This comment by Phal resonates well with this chapter in so far as how exploring a sense of belonging might give some indication as to the personal relations that make up what we call community. For example, Gusfield (1975) argues that a homogeneous culture has often been posited as the mark of community. He suggests that this is marked out by a similarity in language, moralities and common histories that produce a sense of being; a unique and different people. Similarly, Love Brown (2002, p. 6) indicates that 'heterogeneous societies use community to cope with exigencies of life'. She posits that larger social entities are made up of smaller communities that enable face-to-face existence that is the heart of human experience and necessity. Moreover, Kanter's (1972) main emphasis on community is that it cannot exist without some form of strong commitment. Gusfield (1975) appears to describe this as a criterion of common belonging rather than mutual interest.

In this chapter, the idea of a sense of belonging is explored further and links made to a community perception of leadership. While the link between leadership and a sense of belonging has already been made in the literature (see, for instance, De Cremer and Alberts, 2004), it seems the idea of what a sense of belonging is has not been developed further than its generic sense when linking it to leadership. This investigation into views of community will enable a deeper understanding of what is meant by a sense of belonging and how this might give us a deeper understanding of leadership. To do this two case studies of senses of belonging in community are discussed. The case studies emerged from a literature search on 'sense of belonging' and are not academic literature but stories of people's lives growing up in different areas of the UK. The one thing that stood out from both these stories was that they both had 'Sense of Belonging' in the title. This suggested that they would be useful in developing a deeper understanding of this notion. Both cases give biographical accounts of shifting notions of belonging and give us differing accounts of leadership. But first it is worth developing some understanding on research and theory around the topic of sense of belonging.

RESEARCH ON A SENSE OF BELONGING

Most research on a sense of belonging appears to be based in the education sector and takes a distinctly psychological perspective (Faircloth and Hamm, 2005; Freeman et al., 2007; Goodenow, 1993; Goodenow and Grady, 1993; Ma, 2003; Maslow, 1962; Roeser et al., 1996; Young et al., 2004). When reviewing the literature in this area it is interesting to observe the level to which there are strong parallels between findings from sense of belonging research and some aspects of leadership research. Similar to leadership (Chemers et al., 2000; De Cremer et al., 2005; Hill and Ritchie, 1977; Jacobs and McClelland, 1994; McGregor, 1966), sense of belonging has been seen as intrinsically linked to aspects of motivation and achievement (Goodenow, 1993; Roeser et al., 1996) and self-esteem (Ma, 2003). Goodenow and Grady (1993) define sense of belonging as being personally accepted, respected, included and supported and as Ma (2003) points out, there are links to the work of Maslow's (1962) hierarchy of needs, which has also been linked to ideas of leadership and particularly transformational leadership (for example, Burns, 1978). Other research in the area has shown a linked effect whereby if teachers felt a sense of belonging in school, then this transfers onto pupils (Edwards, 1995). A similar effect has been found for transformational leadership and has been termed 'the falling dominoes effect' (Bass et al., 1987). Also, a sense of belonging has been linked to caring relationships either in a religious context (Bales, 1989) or in a university setting (Freeman et al., 2007). Once more this links to leadership as the idea of care is becoming an important focus for ethically orientated ideas of leadership (for example, Ciulla, 2009; Gabriel, forthcoming). As Ciulla (2009) suggests, the duty of a leader is to care for others and take responsibility for them. A community-based perspective, however, would also imply that this 'caring' aspect of leadership is constructed within communities as a mechanism for reducing anxiety.

Last, a sense of belonging also appears to be linked to friendships (Faircloth and Hamm, 2005). Friendships and social networks are investigated further in the next chapter, but it is worth reflecting on the link with belonging highlighted here. Some of these findings and the matched findings with concepts such as transformational leadership seem to suggest that a sense of belonging to a group, organization or community might be seen as a substitute for leadership (for example, Kerr and Jermier, 1978; Manz and Sims, 1980). Substitutes for leadership have been described by Kerr and Jermier (1978) as certain individual, task or organizational variables that act as a substitute for the traditional hierarchical impression of leadership. In a sense, these variables act in the same way as leadership but are sometimes mistaken for leadership. Notions of community, and in this instance a sense of belonging, could be seen to be acting as or constructed as an influencing agent among individuals in a group and labelled as being attributable to leadership from a hierarchical and positional sense. It appears as a result that further research in this area would prove fruitful and in particular developing an understanding of how the two concepts are related, if at all. A critique of this literature is that is seems quite generalist in making sense of a sense of belonging and as I explore later in this chapter, when one opens the subject up through a deep biographical exploration a more entangled idea of a sense of belonging appears that has many interlinking parts. It is this notion of a sense of belonging that is explored in relation to perceptions and constructions of leadership. This entangled notion of a sense of belonging appears to resonate with some researchers that have highlighted a lack of clarity of what constitutes belonging and the role it plays across differing groups (Anderman, 1999; Connell and Wellborn, 1991; Faircloth and Hamm, 2005). It also represents a more sociological idea of belonging through a review of biographical accounts of belonging below.

THE SOCIOLOGY OF BELONGING

... belonging plays a role in connecting individuals to the social.

(May, 2011, p. 368)

The sociology of belonging seems to represent a useful trajectory for leadership studies when connecting with concepts of community. For example, it represents a more dynamic and fluid approach that connects with culture and social change, areas also important in making sense of leadership. May (2011), for instance, defines belonging as being at ease with oneself and our surroundings, but suggests that these experiences of belonging are dynamic and susceptible to change in society. May reviews the literature and features writers who see belonging as a quintessential part of being human, being fully oneself (Miller, 2003), linked to recognizing self in the other (Leach, 2002) and identity (Weeks, 1990). All these areas have also been linked to leadership – being oneself (for example, Goffee and Jones, 2000), links to the other (for example, Cunliffe and Eriksen, 2011) and identity (Ford et al., 2008). Belonging therefore appears to represent an important area of conceptual and empirical investigation for leadership. As May also highlights, through the work of Shotter (1993), there is fluidity to belonging whereby it is not just a collective culture but represents the right to participate in the living tradition of a society. It is this fluidity and cultural connection that this chapter sets out to explore. This chapter, consequently, starts the conceptual journey by looking briefly at two biographical accounts of belonging that may enable further exploration of aspects of self, identity and leadership within society. These two biographical accounts of a sense of belonging come from two communities in the UK, one from the Rhondda Valley in Wales and a second from Hebden Bridge in the north of England.

A SENSE OF BELONGING FROM THE RHONDDA VALLEY

The Rhondda Valley is an area in south Wales in the UK and consists of a community built of coal mining in the Industrial Revolution. It is this context that is explained by Hector Emanuelli (2010) in his autobiography. It is not far into the book that we find a multitude of evidence of aspects of a sense of belonging coming through in his writing. In the first chapter where he gives an account of his early childhood, he describes a fascination with a particular oil painting. This painting is an aesthetic representation of Emanuelli's identity and sense of belonging to the mining community, he describes it as being 'behind a window, . . . brightly coloured and glossy-surfaced . . . prominently displayed on an easel. Illuminated in warm electric, its glowing colours fascinate me!' (p. 1). He goes on to tell us that this painting was his treat on the way home from school and concludes that 'Perhaps it was the work of a hobby painter, possibly a miner working in one of the local collieries' (p. 1). Interestingly, the oil painting starts to become a main focus for the first chapter of Emanuelli's book, later on he also recalls trying to emulate the picture and the 'miner's high Gloss' (p. 4). In this first example, therefore, we might represent a sense of belonging as mimicry or aspiration to be like others we look up to or respect. This is reminiscent of writing around aspirational identity whereby individuals respond to a story-type or template as a desire mechanism for being a particular type of person (Thornborrow and Brown, 2009). In the case of Emanuelli, however, this aspiration is embodied or represented in a symbolic way.

Turning to notions of leadership, one might insinuate that leadership is constructed in organizations as this symbolic representation of aspiration and could then reflect a need to be or belong. While there is an emphasis here on art and aesthetics that links to a sense of belonging, it is the relationships Emanuelli observes that seem to provide a more guiding sense of the link to the community – the idea that the painting was painted by a miner. Here there is a sense of belonging being attached to a certain social and working group – the mining community in the Rhondda Valley – that at this particular time can be seen. The theme of the worker's group also appears to continue in his narrative whereby he recalls the miners' playing a game of 'spitting at the stove'. So the identification with the worker group is evident, but it seems the belongingness also comes from an appreciation of or partaking in the activities they do whether it is games or other activities. Leadership, linked to belonging thus would appear to be heavily imbued into various social groupings and is played out as a game or activity that one plays to represent one's place in that working group. Similarly, Emanuelli also introduces the chapter with an extract from a Dylan Thomas poem. Again, here we see the belongingness being derived from an identification with the aesthetic but herein also there appears a link with a particular Welsh hero.

Throughout the chapter Emanuelli refers to other aspects of belonging, links to his parents, his father's profession as a confectioner and his mother's place in the shop – 'behind the mahogany confectionery counter' (p. 3). What also appears as important is his Ma's use of language, not the Welsh or English language, but the Italian. Further on in the chapter, he refers to the Welsh language and describes a teacher with a 'musical Welsh voice' (p. 5) and the 'tongue twisting Welsh place names' (p. 5). This mixture of language, or as he states 'linguistic confusion' (p. 5), he suggests may be a reason why he suffered from a stutter and had difficulty getting words out. As mentioned above, other individuals besides his parents appear to have had an impact on him feeling part of the community, being inspired by a Welsh teacher, for example.

Further to these ideas of a sense of belonging, it can be seen from Emanuelli's recollection of his early childhood that the senses are important in being able to capture belonging. For instance, he describes his father's confectioners and comes to the conclusion that 'Everything was a long way from the scents and fragrances of a refined Italian bar' (p. 3). Here we again see evidence of his belonging to a certain community in Wales and in the Rhondda, but also to an identity of an Italian in Wales. There are also aspects of comparison and distance in Emanuelli's account. To gain a sense of belonging there appears to be a need here to compare and by comparing the fragrances to Italy gives him a stronger sense of belonging to that distant community and to the present community.

What is evident from this discussion of Emanuelli's biography, therefore, is the importance of multiple belongings. The idea of multiple belongings is recognized in the community literature especially by writers such a Bauman (2000) where there is the recognition of a 'liquid modernity' – where group membership has become more porous and fluid (Delanty, 2003 [2010]). In the case of Emanuelli, there is evidence of multiple belongings, not least the Welsh, the Rhondda, but also the Italian. As can be seen further on in the chapter, this becomes even more complex as we discover that there is also the identity of an Italian in Wales, an Italian in the Rhondda. This also seems to link to Agamben's (1993) idea of 'being-called' as a property of belonging, hence Emanuelli's sense of belonging is drawn out by being called Italian, Welsh or an Italian in Wales.

While one can read into Emanuelli's biography a sense of what is important to gaining a sense of belonging, the book could also be telling us what it is like to be excluded and hence highlight a less desirable aspect to taking a community view of leadership. This is certainly the case when you read Emanuelli's foreword to the book:

> I must confess that there have often been times during the many years of my now long life when I have felt like an outsider . . . I remember feeling very much like an Italian among the Welsh. Then, when I visited my parents' home town in northern Italy at the tender age of seven with my OXO cup and Welsh accent, I felt like a little Welshman – un piccolo gallese – among Italians. Later still, as a teenager in the 1930s when the family moved to England my schoolmates made me feel like a Welshman among the English. The war years were worst: branded as being of 'hostile association' and detained in an internment camp on the Isle of Man, I had never felt so isolated in my life.

This reads more of not having a sense of belonging than having a sense of belonging, in fact it has aspects to that more akin to being in a state of liminality – a state of between-ness – which is another aspect to community discussed later in Chapter 5. This oscillation between belonging and not belonging seems an area of interest that might be informed by ideas of liminality.

A SENSE OF BELONGING FROM HEBDEN BRIDGE

Similar to Emanuelli's reflections on the Rhondda Valley in Wales one does not need to read too far into Paul Barker's (2012) account of an upbringing in a small Yorkshire town in the UK. The thoughts expressed in this section are indeed based solely on his opening preface to his book. In this preface, and similar to Emanuelli's account, Barker talks about how the highest praise in his community was to be seen to be 'a good worker'. Again we see worker values permeating the attachment to a community. This is further elaborated by his comment later on (p. 14) of the town being 'a non-deferential place. No one was called "Sir".' Here we also see a female identity in the sense of belonging, where spinning cloth provided an independence through income for women in the town. Barker goes on to discuss a sense of place and for him he sees buildings 'however beautiful or bizarre' (p. 11) as being important in relaying a sense of place. So once more, similar to Emanuelli (2010), we are drawn to the aesthetic and, particularly, what is seen as aesthetically pleasing (beautiful) and aesthetically curious (bizarre). Picking up on the buildings' aspect of a sense of place Barker goes on to identify particularly with the local bank 'in its fine stone built premises . . .' (p. 12).

We also see evidence of heroes, or in this case heroines, as Barker describes the surrounding area of Hebden Bridge as 'the Bronte end of Yorkshire' (p. 12), referring to the writing sisters of the late nineteenth century – Anne, Emily and Charlotte Bronte. A further hero is mentioned in the guise of the Poet Laureate Ted Hughes, born in the nearby village. Again, here we see an explicit link to the artist reputation of the area as a personal part of his belonging.

Local surnames and family histories are also recalled and interestingly linked to the local geology by the statement 'were as local as the millstone-grit sandstone' (p. 13). This grounding of the surnames into the earth of the surrounding land gives one a sense of what it is to be part of this community, especially when Barker goes on to link the geology back to the psychology of the town – 'the obdurate, utilitarian nature of that rock tells you all you need to know about the psychology of old Hebden' (p. 13). Added to this geological link is the river valley in which the town nestles – the Calder. Last, and interestingly, Barker describes the arrival of 'newcomers' into the area, which he describes as bringing 'new conflict and new hope' (p. 14). Newcomers, therefore, are not only seen as possibly counter-community but also at the same time as bringing a new sense of community.

It appears, then, that in both cases discussed above notions of a sense of belonging are varied, multiple and fluid. The idea of a sense of belonging is also linked to ideas of the aesthetic. It is this aesthetic complexity and fluidity that leadership studies need to connect with to truly understand how, or if, leadership links to a sense of belonging. It also seems worthwhile to reflect on a sense of belonging as social as well as psychological and to uncover the interactive nature of these in having a sense of belonging.

REFLECTIONS FROM THE STORIES OF BELONGING

Findings from this biographical review suggest intricate interplays between various aspects of community such as art, worker groups, heroes and heroines, language, history and geography. The importance in belonging, however, appears not to be these things singularly per se but more the interplay between them. Similar to May's (2011) proposition, these case studies highlight the link sense of belonging has with place and material objects (Downing, 2003; Fortier, 2000; Savage et al., 2005). They also stress another link May (2011) makes to belonging being connected heavily with notions of place (for example, Leach, 2002; Tilley, 1994). Place and space are issues that arise in discussion in Chapter 5, where the book looks at issues of liminality.

There is also evidence of multiple belongings. For example, in the story from the Rhondda Valley of Hector Emanuelli, born to Italian parents and as the story unfolds there is evidence of multiple belongings, not least the Welsh, the Rhondda, but also the Italian. This becomes even more complex as we discover that there is also the identity of an Italian in Wales, an Italian in the Rhondda and a Welsh identity in Italy when visiting family. This implies not only multiple belongings but fluid and changing ideas of hierarchies of belonging (May, 2011) whereby sometimes one sense of belonging is more important than another within particular contexts. It is these complexities that leadership studies fail to recognize.

When taking this biographical perspective, we might see leadership linked to belonging as being heavily imbued into various social groupings and is enacted as a game or activity that one plays to represent one's place in that working group. One might also suggest that leadership is constructed in organizations as a symbolic representation of social aspiration and could consequently reflect a need to be or belong. In relation to this point, however, we must not forget that belonging is an inter-subjective experience where we are continuously claiming belonging that others either accept or reject (May, 2011). Using the biographical cases above only allows us to see the claim to belonging and multiple belonging, whether this is accepted or rejected remains an area for further examination.

Last, and from a more critical domain, there is evidence herein that a sense of belonging could be viewed as a 'substitute' for leadership (Kerr and Jermier, 1978). There is little evidence in these biographical accounts for 'leadership', it appears more around connection to a groups or environment. One thus might question whether leadership is being constructed in communities. Certainly key heroic individuals are mentioned – artists, poets, teachers, parents, but these individuals are not described as leaders, so it is debatable to what extent one can construct leadership from a sense of belonging. The role of leaders and leadership are then a part of the development of a sense of belonging in communities themselves. A further critical point is that belonging and a sense of belonging should not be seen as positive at the expense of not belonging. As May (2011) points out, not belonging can harbour positive feelings as much as belonging, consequently linking leadership to notions of not belonging may also provide a fruitful line of inquiry for further research.

SUMMARY

This chapter has reviewed the literature on a sense of belonging and suggested leadership studies should make closer connections to fluid and complex concept of a sense of belonging and not take the concept as a catch-all phrase within empirical research. The chapter has explored the inherent fluidity and complexity of sociological inter-pretations of a sense of belonging through two case studies. These case studies are not exhaustive and are there as a means to exemplify how leadership studies can gain a deeper insight into leadership and a sense of belonging through a community perspective. For instance, from the short reflection on these stories multiple and contextualized notions of identity were portrayed. It seems leadership studies can take this form of exploring leadership from a socially constructed view to gain insight into the phenomenon set within community and society ideals. As colleagues and I have suggested elsewhere (Edwards et al., forthcoming b), gathering life stories of leaders and analysing these stories similar to Ciulla's (2013) analysis of Mandela could also benefit the study of leadership. This will enable a broader and deeper appreciation of the intricacies of such concepts as sense of belonging when linked to leadership.

3. Leadership, friendship and social networks

> Friendship is a powerful weapon in the real politics of decision-making
> and it would be naive not to recognize it.
> (Norris, 2001, p. 8, cited in French, 2007, p. 262)

This chapter explores concepts of friendship and social networks and how these concepts inform our knowledge of community, and, in turn, our knowledge of leadership. As shall be seen, this is an area of significant research in the leadership field already, but further reflection on the topic from an explicit community outlook appears warranted. To start it is worth taking Etzioni's (1993) critical standpoint who advises that one of the main criticisms of community perspectives is that concepts of community are vague and fuzzy and that ideas of strong communities curb individual freedoms. One must recognize, then, the 'in group' and 'out group' nature as a core element of potential exclusion within the idea of a strong community and hence the criticism of 'tribalism' that can be levelled at communitarian ideals. Personal communities, as Phal (2000) suggests, can be inward looking, conservative and resistant to change. He goes on to propose that in some circumstances friendships can be dangerous, such as in instances of political purges. Community as a concept and those built on strong friendships may not, thus, always be a good thing. What is more, Etzioni sees communities as social webs of people that draw on common values to bind them together. Phal (2000) warns of becoming too romanticized by informal groups and these types of close groups are not always beneficial as highlighted above. It is this idea of social, friendship and work networks, though, that is discussed in more detail below.

FRIENDSHIP AND SOCIAL NETWORKS

Taylor (1982) has insinuated that communities make widespread friendship possible. Similarly, Phal (2000), drawing on Aristotle, suggests friendships presuppose a form of community and every generation rethinks the idea of friendship in its own terms. Friendship therefore is a fluid concept (Vernon, 2010). The picture of community based on friendship is ever-changing and we can only capture a snapshot at a time. This chapter represents one of these snapshots and attempts to relate it to a similar changing concept – leadership. It seems that friendship and social networks are a key component of community (Delanty, 2003 [2010]), and as we shall discover below also a key component of leadership and hence merit a deeper appreciation.

The haven provided by social networks in modern society seems to be becoming increasingly more important. Whether this is due to the dominance of large formal organizations in society, as predicted by Gans (1988), or the increase in technology for networking, the link with leadership and community seems significant. In parallel, the exploration of leadership away from organizational hierarchical structures appears to be gaining ground in the literature. This can be evidenced from the work on distributed leadership, reviewed in the introduction to this book, but also work looking at leadership in social networks (Balkundi and Kilduff, 2006). For example, Balkundi and Kilduff advocate that an understanding, appreciation and active management of social networks is important for leaders. Conversely they also suggest that an understanding of social networks can help to understand how leaders emerge and hold power in organizations. They go on to use social network theory (Lord and Emrich, 2001) and Leader-Member Exchange (LMX) (for example, Graen and Uhl-Bien, 1995; Sparrowe and Liden, 1997, 2005) to make the link between social networks and leadership more explicit. While recognizing this work as an important shift in understanding leadership in organizations, this chapter concentrates on the core concept within social networks – friendship. Not least as this is also an under-researched area within leadership studies, but also in light of its clear link to notions of community. Maffesoli (1996), for instance, explores networks of acquaintances and circles of friends in his book *The Time of Tribes.* His book paints a picture of modernity that reflects the 'being together' of everyday life (Shields, 1996) that is underexplored in leadership studies.

When exploring what friendship means, Phal (2000, p. 17) indicates that:

> ... friends are your accumulated history, they hold you up and remind you who you are and insist on who it is you remain.

This is similar to the view of Little (1993), who suggests three differing ideas of friendship. 'Communicating Friendship' is about the mutual discovery of identity and meaning, built on interactions that revolve around hope, reinventing the future through the reinterpretation of the past. 'Familiar Friendship', he proposes, is a form of friendship that is an extension of the family and is built upon loyalty and offers help, comfort, continuity and stability. Last, 'Social Friendship' is based on organized social relations and is a friendship seen within workmates and colleagues. This latter type of friendship offers shared interests, a common cause and comradeship and is built on solidarity. Little goes on to describe friendship as being ourselves with others, which is the sub-title to his book. He paints a picture of friendship that is inherently liminal (a topic discussed further in Chapter 5) and states:

> Friendship is sociologically in-between – not quite society's, not quite ours – and it is psychologically transitional, located somewhere between friends, not in one or the other of them.
>
> (Little, 1993, p. 58)

This statement could also help to describe leadership socially in-between and reinforces relational (Cunliffe and Eriksen, 2011; Uhl-Bien, 2006) and liminal (Hawkins and Edwards, forthcoming) notions of leadership that are emerging in the literature.

As Phal (2000) highlights, friendship networks, certainly in the West, are becoming more central to society than other forms of networks such as work or geographically based networks. He goes on to suggest that the styles and symbols of contemporary culture are increasingly mediated through friendship. To exemplify this Phal observes that in contemporary society magazines and fashion link more readily to friends than they do to family. This shifting ground therefore has a bearing on communities and organizations alike, especially given the growing influence of social networking media through communication tools such as Facebook and Twitter. Hence the link between friendship and leadership seems to be a growing concern for organizations and society. Indeed and linking back to the previous chapter, Vernon (2010) recommends that friendship at work provides us with a sense of belonging. Vernon goes on to suggest that the workplace is one of the best sources of friends as well as one of the most desirable places to have friends. He does warn, however, that these are in the first instances built on utility, an issue developed more deeply later in the chapter.

Discussions of friendship in organization studies (French, 2007, 2008; French et al., 2009) imply a shift towards non-hierarchical perceptions of leadership. It is a review of these areas that represent this particular chapter, but in line with the theme of the book, the chapter draws heavily on the community literature to inform potentially new areas of research and theory development.

LEADERSHIP AND FRIENDSHIP

> The warmth of friendship is the warmth of a blanket, wrapped and clasped, but always in danger of blowing away, or being torn from my back by another, or by fate itself.
>
> (French et al., 2009, p. 152)

Friendship is seen as holding society together (Broadie and Rowe, 2002, cited in French et al., 2009) and hence is important when considering community in relation to leadership. Recent work by colleagues such as Robert French, Peter Case and Jonathan Gosling has highlighted critical and ethical issues in organizational leadership through the lens of notions of friendship and betrayal, the oscillating shadow side of friendship (French et al., 2009). French (2008), for example, compares ideas of leadership to classical and Western friendship traditions. A key point he makes in his work is the seemingly paradoxical nature of organizational leadership when viewed through the friendship lens. For instance, in contemporary organizations a leader's friendship networks are seen as private and even viewed with suspicion to the extent that legal frameworks are set up in organizations to counter the influence of such networks. As French points out, though, by taking a classical friendship tradition a leader without a strong supportive friendship network would be viewed with suspicion (see French, 2007 for a review of notions of friendship and organization theory). Friendship, however, is seen as a problem in organizations (Fraisse, 1974) and the political value of friendship has become hidden (Spencer and Phal, 2006) in contemporary organizational life (French et al., 2009). French et al. (2009) go on to suggest that if and when friendship is explicit in organizations it is viewed with suspicion and mistrust.

In 2008, however, French also pointed to the importance of friendship in leading organizations especially when drawing on ideas of 'friends of' organizations, such as Friends of the Earth or the Quakers – the Society of Friends. Here we see the notion of friendship as the driving force in the creation of, and ongoing running of, these types of organizations. French also discusses the creation of start-up organizations such as Aardman Animations and Innocent Drinks. Again here, at least in the initial set-up there is a strong impression of friendship that drives the organization forward and lends itself to the way that leadership is viewed in the organization. Both organizations, French (2008) explains, were drawn from a matrix of friends. He goes on to observe that many small creative organizations are initiated in this manner. Friendship in this case, therefore, is leadership. Going further back, French also uses the case of St Anselm (Fiske, 1961) to highlight the very foundations of friendship being the key to strategic leadership. St Anselm was a Benedictine monk and philosopher who become Archbishop of Canterbury around the turn of the twelfth century and aspects of his leadership in this role are explicitly linked to what we would recognize as friendship. French (2008) suggests that this case exemplifies Aristotle's model of friendship. He then uses the case to underline an ultimate paradox of contemporary organization leadership whereby the modern discourse is of the importance of networking, partnerships and stakeholder management, but it is hard to imagine the close ally of friendship being openly recommended as an important asset to the organization. Yet in terms of historical context, philosophical consideration and community perspectives, it appears inherently important, yet also at the same time problematic to notions of leadership.

THE POLITICS OF FRIENDSHIP

Developing ideas of friendship further and looking into the work of Derrida (1988) brings about a realization of the politics of friendship that also seems to have an interesting connection to the leadership literature. Derrida stresses the double exclusion of the feminine in the philosophical paradigm of friendship where there is an exclusion of friendship between women and between a man and a woman. As Phal highlights, traditionally friendship is seen as a masculine virtue that was about developing enduring same-sex bonds (Tiger, 1969). This appears reflective of the masculinization of leadership (Ford, 2010), which to one extent represents male managers' views on leadership as evoking homoerotic desire in followers (Harding et al., 2011). Harding and colleagues go on to conclude that charisma arises out of this sexual desire to seduce followers to achieve organizational goals. Along these lines Derrida (1997) goes on to emphasize the possibility of a narcissistic 'virtuality' to friendship whereby the relationship is projected from one person to another (cited in French et al., 2009). This is reminiscent of notions of charismatic leadership and the attribution of charisma onto leaders from followers (for example, Conger and Kanungo, 1987, 1998). Also, this underlines issues around the level of friendliness we might expect from those we see as leaders. For example, a recent small-scale research project using student perceptions of leadership advocated that some would-be followers expect a level of friendliness from their leaders while others expect a degree of separation, to a larger or smaller extent (Curtis, 2013). This distance or level of friendship between organizational members and those seen as leaders may be linked to the related concept explored by French and colleagues (2009) – betrayal.

FRIENDSHIP, BETRAYAL AND LEADERSHIP LEARNING

> ... betrayal is an essential element of leadership and organisational change.
>
> (Krantz, 2006, p. 222)

Building on the quote above, this section looks at the role betrayal plays in leading in organizations and why it might be one of the most important areas to concentrate on in any leadership development experience. Krantz, for instance, suggests that betrayal is inherent in organizations and not just the negative forms of betrayal such as corruption and immoral acts but also, and maybe more importantly, 'virtuous betrayal'. Krantz describes virtuous betrayal as when one must betray loyalty and trust in pursuit of a task. Herein, therefore, Krantz relates back to leadership as virtuous betrayal tends to sit between the need for change and the need for stability. An interesting take that Krantz has is that the common projection of leadership, that of communicating a vision (for example, Bass, 1985; Saskin, 1988), is a form of virtuous betrayal as it reveals a form of truth. Bringing this truth into reality, he goes on to say, destabilizes the equilibrium and emotional states attached to that status quo, hence a form of betrayal. He insinuates that when forces of change collide with the status quo betrayal is inevitable. This is why he proposes that leadership learning is centrally about coping with betrayal both internally and externally. Internally in the sense of leaders coping emotionally with betraying those that have loyalty and trust in them and externally in the sense of coping with the emotionality of those being betrayed. Working with forgiveness, Krantz endorses, is a root to developing leaders around notions of betrayal in organizations.

Interestingly, French et al. (2009) propose that the relationship between friendship and betrayal starts with betrayal and that betrayal is an inevitable experience of human life that may contribute to the moment when our sense of 'I' begins. Here there seems to be a link with ideas of leadership development, self-development and being oneself. For some time leadership development has been synonymous with self-development in that leadership development is regarded as finding oneself and once this has been accomplished one can lead others (for example, Bennis, 1984, 1989; Edwards et al., 2002; Goffee and Jones, 2000). If this is the case, then it appears important to include discussions of betrayal in leadership learning and development interventions, to discuss betrayal by others but also betrayal of oneself when goals and objectives are not met. Also 'being oneself' seems related to notions of friendship, especially if we take Lewis's (1961) idea of friendship, as cited in French et al. (2009). Lewis sees friendship as one of 'four loves' and sees close friendship as being when we can feel truly free to be ourselves. Little (1993) also proposes friendship as being oneself with others, which resonates with comments on leadership development and self-development evidenced above, but also adds an explicit friendship angle to such notions.

It also serves to problematize issues of leadership development as self-development. For example, one can question the level to which we as leaders can actually be ourselves in the way promoted by popular discourse in leadership studies. This links to the issues highlighted above by French and colleagues in the tension of leadership and friendship within organizational settings and begs the question how close should leaders get to followers? And if they are not close to followers, how can they truly be themselves? This conundrum reflects concerns in the literature regarding the level to which a leader should be truly 'authentic' (for example, Clarke et al., 2013). It appears that contemporary writing on leadership is encouraging us to be close and this rings true with historical views of friendship as described by French and others, but organizational politics and procedures seem to battle against this in the interests of equality and parity. This therefore suggests that it is unreasonable to expect leaders to be so close to followers as to be friends, and in turn unreasonable to imply that leaders can be 'themselves', owing to the pressures of their roles in the crucible of an organization. If, however, leadership is seen through the lens of friendship then it becomes perfectly acceptable to be close and oneself. Herein, then, leadership development programmes or learning interventions need to explore this tension as part of the paradigm they are setting for individuals and organizations. This would redress something that has resulted from the splitting off of friendship into 'private life' (MacIntyre, 1984 [1991]), the omission of a discourse of political friendship from management and leadership training (French et al., 2009).

LEADERSHIP, FRIENDSHIP AND ETHICS

In reviewing the literature around friendship French (2007) also points to an ethical dimension, citing Aristotle's writings (Blum, 1980; Stern-Gillet, 1995) being in some part devoted to friendship. Ethics is becoming an increasing concern for leadership scholars (for example, Brown and Treviño, 2006; Brown et al., 2005; Ciulla, 2004a, 2004b, 2012; Ciulla and Forsyth, 2011; Cunha et al., 2010; Knights and O'Leary, 2006; Mendonca and Kanungo, 2007; Treviño et al., 2000, 2003) and is discussed in more detail in Chapter 7. Suffice to say here, however, that these ideas of ethical leadership and notions of friendship from a community perspective appear, at least in philosophical terms, to be intrinsically linked. As Phal (2000, p. 22) highlights:

Virtuous friends enlarge and extend other's moral experience. The friends are bound together, becoming, as it were, each other, as they recognize each other's moral excellence.

Further on in his book Phal (p. 78) also describes this as friends becoming a second self and suggests the 'self' is partly a product of friendship. He draws on Aristotle to put forward that when we choose a friend, we choose a second self. Phal proposes that what we receive back from friends is not a reflection of ourselves, but an interpretation and that friendship is important for self-sufficiency. As Little (1993, p. 245) stresses, friends are 'agents of self-discovery – they show us who we are when we are not at home . . . they help others to see us and us to see ourselves'. If guided by ideas of friendship when choosing leaders, therefore, we are identifying an interpretation of a second self, one that gives us confidence to be ourselves. The suggestion could also be that leaders and followers become indistinguishable within what is seen as moral action. As Phal hints at, friendship can be seen as a metaphor for morality. Hence the drawing together of roles in a community along the lines of friendship and mutual moral understanding can push notions of leadership to be deconstructed and potentially disappear. Or alternatively, ideas of leadership and followership become metaphors for morality in organizational settings.

Interestingly, Phal highlights issues of friendship that are superficial and insincere, such as that of colleagues and neighbours. Herein, then, the nature of leadership, in organizations at least, appears to serve towards a superficial, insincere level of friendship. For instance, notions of leadership in contemporary literature appear to oscillate on a tension between the structured masculine idea linked to distance and more feminine ideals of closeness. This is even seen within the same concept in some cases, for example, in inspirational motivation, the communication of vision (arguably an inherently social distancing process) and individualized consideration (the close mentoring of a team member), both aspects of the wider perception of transformational leadership (see Bass and Riggio, 2006). Also, a more critical view would see leadership as a constructed idea for the control of organizational members. Here leadership would be seen to try and be 'friendly' for the purposes of delivering a task. This is similar to Bellah's (1985) description of Carnegie's (1936) view of friendship, which was an occupational tool for entrepreneurs to be used as an instrument within a competitive society (cited in Phal, 2000, p. 46). Notions of leadership consequently could be seen in this more critical way as being there to develop pseudo-friendship (Vernon, 2010) in organizations for the purposes of succeeding in increasingly competitive times, a source of competitive advantage. As Phal (2000, p. 90) suggests:

> . . . communicating friendship is trivialized and demeaned by the superficial glad-handedness of much corporate culture. The ever-spiralling, first-name-calling networkers are the enemies of true friendship. They take up our time and lure us to the popular crowd at the symbolic bars of life.

Leadership, therefore, is in danger of becoming a type of lure away from true friendship in organizations. Moreover, the description of a socialite by Phal (2000, p. 69) also warns of leaders linking to ideas of friendship in a superficial and insincere way:

> The socialite with 'hundreds of friends' has no friends: she has many refractions of an ever-changing kaleidoscopic self with no centre. Such 'friends' disappear when the patronage or social advantage decline.

Is this the tension of leadership in organization – to make friends in a superficial way? But if distance does play an important role in leading (for example, see Grint, 2010b) then this is maybe the best we can expect as leaders. This also speaks of societies driven to romanticize leadership and if we do individualize those seen as leaders and place a heroic status upon them then we are, as Phal suggests, refracting (or in more contemporary terms 'fracking') their 'self' at the expense of this hunt for celebrity.

Last, there is a link back to characterization first discussed in Chapter 1, as Phal (2000, p. 112) advises:

> Having a close, character making friend, based on open communication, is likely to be far more significant and important for an individual's future development than simply being surrounded by peers – crowd, the gang, the mates of whatever.

From this quote, therefore, reference can be made to the deep rooted nature of characterization in social interaction. Even within close relationships, such as friendship, our characters are formed. It is not surprising then that we also characterize those in organizations we see as leaders; this may be a signifier of the closeness to which leader-follower relationships are developed. From my experience of leadership development programmes it is interesting to note the 'life-changing' discourse present among those having gone through such programmes. One could argue that a root of this discourse may lie in the friendships developing on these programmes out of groups of peers and colleagues and in some instances from total strangers. The notion of leadership development consequently may not be about self-development but more about friendship development. Leadership development and learning consequently should be orientated towards this idea of self as a reflection in friendship.

SUMMARY

This chapter has looked briefly into the notion of friendship and its shadow side, betrayal, and linked them to ideas of leadership. What appears as important is not just the link between leadership and friendship and the tense space within which these ideas reside in organizational realities but also the importance of betrayal, not just to our understanding of the emergence of leadership in organizations but also its ongoing development. From this chapter it is clear that further research in non-traditional settings, that is, those outside the workplace and in social settings, seems to be needed in leadership studies. In addition, Aristotle's categories of friendship (reviewed in French, 2007), as utility (a useful bond between people), as pleasure or congeniality (an affectionate bond between people) and as a 'true friendship' (a higher level bond between people that is seen as more important than oneself) appear to be a useful starting point to explore the way leadership might be constructed as a discourse. Also, and related, it seems merited to put forward that further research also needs to be developed regarding related concepts to friendship, such as partnership, fellowship and kinship (Phal, 2000). Last, and while the topic has only briefly been cited in this chapter, the idea of leadership in social networks, as highlighted by Balkundi and Kilduff (2006), needs further research. In their paper, Balkundi and Kilduff (2006, p. 420) cite the work of Brass et al. (2004, p. 800) who state: 'little empirical work has been done on leadership and social networks'. This needs to change and especially in light of the contemporary working world being cross-fertilized with the social world through media, information technology and mobile working. Herein, therefore, the suggestion would be to develop further research around virtual networks and social groups linked to leadership.

4. Leadership, symbolism and aesthetics

> Community exists in the minds of its members, and should not be confused with geographic or sociographic assertions of 'fact'. By extension, the distinctiveness of communities and, thus, the reality of their boundaries, similarly lies in the mind, in the meanings which people attach to them, not in their structural forms.
> (Cohen, 1985, p. 98)

This chapter looks at the symbolic representation and interpretation of community and the meaning attached, as Cohen suggests above. This, in turn, relates to the study of leadership. For instance, leadership has been linked with organizational culture (for example, Schein, 2004) and national culture (for example, Den Hartog and Dickson, 2004) for some time, but it tends to lack integration with symbolism. For example, there are a number of cross-cultural leadership studies, such as GLOBE (for example, Chhokar et al., 2007; House et al., 2004), based on quantitative, normative views of leadership styles, behaviours and categories but this then misses the aesthetic nuances evident in culture. This chapter therefore expands on these areas by adding theoretical depth to the culture and leadership relationship through an artistic and aesthetic lens. It reviews the growing body of literature around art, aesthetics and leadership. The chapter then looks at symbolic notions of community and links these to leadership and finally more postmodern ideas of aesthetics and community are reviewed and related to the field of leadership studies.

ART, AESTHETICS AND LEADERSHIP

In the literature on leadership there is a burgeoning focus on artistic and aesthetic interpretations, methodologies and pedagogies (for example, Acevedo, 2011; Barry and Meisiek, 2010; Bathurst and

Monin, 2010; Bathurst et al., 2010; Gayá Wicks and Rippin, 2010; Griffey and Jackson, 2010; Guillet de Monthoux et al., 2007; Hansen and Bathhurst, 2011; Hansen et al., 2007; Howard, 1996; Ladkin, 2006, 2008; Ladkin and Taylor, 2010; Ropo and Sauer, 2008; Ropo et al., 2002; Schyns et al., 2013; Springborg, 2010; Sutherland, 2013; Sutherland and Walravens, 2011; Woodward and Funk, 2010). This chapter takes this body of literature and research as inspiration to delve deeper into leadership as artistic or aesthetic representation. Within the literature on leadership there has been a link with beauty in the sense of 'leading beautifully' (Ladkin, 2008). Ladkin, in this paper, expresses the need for 'leaders' to enact 'leadership' through beautiful representation, they act and behave within an appreciation of beauty. In this chapter I reflect on beauty in a wider sense and see beauty as leadership. While Ladkin is working towards a notion of leadership as symbolism, I shall argue that by taking a community perspective we might develop this link further. For instance, the link between leadership and cultural aspects such as symbolism was identified back in 1973 by James Downton who identified how leaders and leadership make links with historical heroes, to religious principles and ceremonies to highlight the values to which they espouse. Second, Downton also made links to leaders maintaining equilibrium by developing new symbols, responding to latent senti-ments, prejudices or fears (Downton, 1973, pp. 12–13). This view on revolutionary leadership is where the more contemporary ideas of transformational leadership were first developed. These notions of transformational leadership from the 1980s (for example, Bass, 1985; Bennis and Nanus, 1985), however, appear to have lost the link with symbolism. This chapter hopes to rejuvenate this initial observation by Downton, but also to develop these ideas further by drawing more explicitly on the community literature. In its most extreme potential, then, leadership is symbolic in nature.

SYMBOLS, RITUALS AND LEADERSHIP

> . . . symbols are essentially involved in social process.
>
> (Turner, 1967, p. 20)

From his anthropological work, Turner sees ritual as distinct phases in social processes whereby groups become adapted to their external environment. He also advises that symbols instigate social action and are stimuli for emotion and serve as representations of the unity and continuity of social groups. He talks of three types of symbol; referential, instrumental and ritual. He describes 'referential' symbols as things like oral speech, writing, flags and signalling. 'Instrumental' symbols are more contextually bound in that they must be seen in terms of their wider context, whereas ritual symbols strike deeper into the roots of the unconscious. He highlights that ritual symbols refer to what is normative, general and characteristic of unique individuals and relate to community aspects such as basic needs and shared values. He goes on to imply that the structure and properties of ritual symbols can be gained from three classes of data; an external form consisting of observable characteristics; interpretations from specialists and laymen; and significant contexts that can be worked out by anthropologists. First and foremost, therefore, if leadership is linked somehow to rituals and symbols, these sources of data appear important for further investigation and, especially the latter, as is the point of this chapter and in the next chapter on liminality.

Among other writers, this chapter takes inspiration from the writing of Anthony Cohen (1985). In his work Cohen looks at the symbolic construction of community. He draws on earlier writings by philosophers and anthropologists such as Durkheim (1964), Geertz (1975, 1983), Turner (1967, 1969) and Weber (1948). These foundations of literature and philosophy enable Cohen (1985) to develop a sense of community as built on symbolic interpretation. While some writers see boundaries as a key element of community (for example, Love Brown, 2002), Cohen seems to go further by seeing the symbolic representation of community lying within boundaries. He takes a relational view here whereby community boundary represents the plurality of concurrent similarity and difference, the opposition of one community against another, the beginning and end of community. He recognizes the statutory boundaries of community such as those created by race, religion and language. He also recognizes that these symbolic representations of community are as much open to interpretation and exist in the minds of their beholders. He uses a quote by Geertz to illustrate this point, 'man is an animal suspended in webs of significance he himself has spun' (Geertz, 1975, p. 5).

Cohen thus appears to take a social construction standpoint by proposing that social interaction is the transaction of meanings.

These meanings, he adds, are also subjective interpretations made within the terms characteristic of a given society – influenced by language, ecology, traditions of belief and ideology and so on. He also appears to suggest a relational view whereby these interpretations are changeable in response to interactions, both among individuals and between the society as a whole and those across its boundaries. He highlights that the vehicles of such interpretations are symbols. Symbols permit interpretation and provide scope for interpretative manoeuvres and they provide a medium through which individuals can experience and express their attachment to a society without compromising their individuality. He reminds us that the symbols of community are mental constructs; they provide people with the means to make meaning and that symbols are effective because they are imprecise. They are not content-less as part of their meaning is subjective. They become, then, a useful way for people to speak a common language, behave in apparently similar ways, participate in the same rituals and so on without, Cohen says, subjecting themselves to the tyranny of orthodoxy.

These perspectives on community are interesting given the increased focus on leadership as meaning making (Smircich and Morgan, 1982) and sense making (Pye, 2005), as being socially constructed (Grint, 2005a; Grint and Jackson, 2010) and relational (Cunliffe and Eriksen, 2011). The ideas of Cohen, however, add to this literature by suggesting a number of differing interpretations that can be taken regarding leadership from a community, context and cultural outlook. These interpretations appear not to be mutually exclusive but constructed either in competition, as a tension, or in parallel. For example, from Cohen's ideas, one could quite easily see the construction of leadership in community as part of the interpretation of boundary, indeed as a symbol of boundary. Still, one could also see quite easily that leadership could be constructed as the boundary itself. These various interpretations are explored in more detail below.

LEADERSHIP AS A MASK: CONTRIBUTING TO THE SYMBOLIC COMMUNITY BOUNDARY

From the discussion regarding Cohen's work, it seems reasonable to imply that the construction of terms such as leadership would

contribute to the symbolic representations of community boundaries. We label people and process as leaders, leadership, followers
and followership to demarcate community to which we belong. This
has resonance with ideas of 'in-group' and 'out-group' but these
terms are also constructed through differing language and indeed
have a deeper attachment with our cultural identity. As Cohen
highlights, symbolism in boundary maintenance creates a sense of
belonging and identity, and by the same token, a difference from
others. Within this, however, we also see a more uncomfortable side
to taking a community view whereby leadership as a symbolic part of
community boundary welcomes but also ostracizes individuals and
groups. There is an element here of 'them' and 'us'. Which has been
an issue with concepts such as 'in-groups' and 'out-groups'. But this
may also reflect the harsh nature of society and that we must accept
this is a social process with which we live with and within. Cohen
also reminds us that the symbolic construction of community and its
boundaries are relational not absolute, they mark out communities
in relation to others. In this sense, therefore, leadership is relational
much the same as all social identities are, collective or individual.
The role of constructed concepts of leadership and followership is
to mark out boundaries between communities but also to identify
the relationship the community has with other communities. This
builds on earlier ideas of relational leadership (for example, Cunliffe
and Eriksen, 2011) that reflect the relational nature of the leader-
follower relationship; herein, though, there is a further relational
element to leadership: that of its relation to other forms of leadership
of other communities.

Cohen also indicates that symbolism constitutes the boundary
between the mundane and the sacred. A link can be drawn
here between ideas of the construction of leadership as extra-
ordinarization of the mundane (Alvesson and Sveningsson, 2003)
and ideas of leadership as sacred (Grint, 2010b). Symbolism in this
boundary maintenance role creates a sense of belonging and identity. This is further evidence of the construction of leadership being
a symbol of boundary maintenance, especially when considering the
work of Ford and colleagues (2008) around the notion of leadership as identity. In addition, the link back to a sense of belonging
discussed in Chapter 2 might be in the form of boundary maintenance. Leadership acts as a sense of belonging as it is constructing
boundaries in social groupings. As Cohen goes on to state:

> The community in this regard is a cluster of symbolic and ideological
> map references with which the individual is socially orientated.
>
> (Cohen, 1985, p. 57)

Moreover the idea that leadership is constructed to contribute to the symbolic representation of community and its boundary, leadership could also be the boundary. Here we draw on the idea or analogy of a mask. Cohen describes the boundary as the mask presented by the community to the outside world. Is this mask the construction of leadership? Is leadership constructed not just as a piece of the boundary but the boundary itself? For instance, Cohen describes how symbolism also continually reinforces cultural boundaries of the community by reconstituting its tradition. Then leadership is constructed as this, as a means by which we can reconstitute tradition in communities. Leadership, then, could also be ritual.

LEADERSHIP AS RITUAL

There are other symbolic representations that can be developed from Cohen's (1985) work that could relate to leadership. For example, Cohen through the work of Geertz (1975) describes how rituals in society serve to reflect what society wants and needs. Cohen describes a cockfight in a Balinese village. The cockfight, it is concluded,

> ... represents a fantasy, a picture of what Balinese society might be like
> if it was not trammelled by the rigidities of status, the constraints of
> convention and of the tightly controlled behaviour.
>
> (Cohen, 1985, p. 68)

Leadership, in this paradigm, therefore, could reflect a community's aspiration for structure and meaning. This appears to link into suggestions of leadership being an empty signifier whereby leadership does not signify anything specific but creates conditions of possibility for differing meanings (Ford et al., 2008; Kelly, 2014). Similarly, this perspective resonates with leadership ultimately being a process for meaning making (Smircich and Morgan, 1982). This could also link to leadership being some form of fantasy that is played out in society, again to reflect a symbolic representation of order. This links to boundary maintenance. As Cohen highlights:

We have found that as the structural basis of the boundary become undermined or weakened as a consequence of social change, so people resort increasingly to symbolic behaviour to reconstitute the boundary.

(Cohen, 1985, p. 70)

So leadership, in this sense, could be described as symbolic behaviour serving various fantasies of order and chaos, and hence this may explain the exhaustive link with change, whether it be the creation of change (for example, Kotter, 1990) or the resistance to change (Levay, 2010; Zoller and Fairhurst, 2007).

LEADERSHIP AS AESTHETIC FRILL

Last, in this chapter, Leach (1954) identifies the 'aesthetic frill', the ritual and symbolism with which societies embellish their routine and technical behaviour, as expressing the essence and, therefore, the distinctiveness of the society. Cohen goes on to assert that within these aesthetics lie the 'ethical rules' of society. This links the symbolic with ethical discussions held later in the book, but also points to the construction of leadership in community as a form of 'aesthetic frill'. We are continuously reminded that leadership is a guiding symbol of ethicality (for example, Mendonca and Kanungo, 2007), toxicity (for example, Lipman-Blumen, 2005) or being bad (for example, Kellerman, 2004) and if we take leadership to be a symbolic construction in society, then it could be described as an aesthetic frill, being a ritual in our organizations, communities and societies that sets roots in behaviour and highlights distinctiveness from one community to the next. The idea of leadership as 'aesthetic frill' seems an interesting concept that could hold information regarding the reason for leadership in community but also to explain differences between leadership according to culture and language. This could be an interesting frame for further research around leadership, but the chapter now turns towards more postmodern perspectives on community and aesthetics, reflecting on ideas such as the reflexive community and the imagined community.

REFLEXIVE COMMUNITY

Lash (1994) uses ideas of reflexive modernity to explore ideas and
notions of community. Lash goes on to hint that community is
based on meaning and draws on aesthetic ideals. He reflects on the
idea of *Imagined Communities* by Benedict Anderson (1983 [2006]).
Anderson (1983 [2006]) proposes that nations can be described as
imagined political communities. They are imagined in the sense that
most people within a nation will never meet nor know most of their
fellow members of the state. Yet there is, in the minds of the inhabitants, an image of a communion for which those involved in the nation
are willing to die for. Anderson draws on Gellner's comment that:

> Nationalism is not the awakening of nation to self-consciousness: it
> invents nations where they do not exist.
>
> (Gellner, 1964, p. 169)

There is a similar observation now being discussed within the leadership literature (Edwards, forthcoming) and relates to perceptions of
worldliness and leadership underlined in the introduction to this book
(for example, Turnbull, 2009). This body of literature recognizes the
fragility of nations as a basis of cross-cultural comparison and the
connection that these ideas have to others such as globalization –
'nationalism's marriage to internationalism' (Anderson, 1983 [2006],
p. 207). It does suggest, however, a closer notion of community
at a more local and contextual level and that this should also be a
basis for leadership research and theoretical engagement. Anderson
relates to this focus in leadership studies as he indicates that 'all
communities larger than primordial villages of face-to-face contact
(and perhaps even these) are imagined' (1983 [2006], p. 6). He goes
on to suggest that communities need to be distinguished by the style
to which they are imagined.

Leadership studies, therefore, may take this as a basis for reflection
and develop research that investigates how leadership is imagined in
the local context. Indeed Anderson takes us back to the importance
of language, where he highlights the sacred nature of language in
the classical communities of the ancient world. Here, he also draws
our attention to the importance of symbols in other languages, as
he advises that both the Arabic and Chinese 'characters create a
community out of signs, not sounds' (1983 [2006], p. 13). Herein,

then, there is a connection to be made between earlier chapters in this book and between the importance of language and the symbolic or aesthetic – an avenue we are yet to explore within leadership studies. This reflects the Westernization of the leadership literature and the lack of recognition in the West, as Anderson points out, of the non-arbitrariness of signs and symbols. This brings us back to the work of Lash (1994) whereby he relates aesthetic reflexivity to ideas of society and community. He draw on ideas of the imagined community and suggests that communities are thus 'merely associations of atomized individuals' (Lash, 1994, p. 144). In this sense he advocates that to access any notion of the 'we' and thus perceptions of community, researchers and theorists should not deconstruct but hermeneutically interpret to give access to the ontological foundations of aesthetic individualism. Doing this will, in turn, he suggests, give some understanding of shared meanings of community – 'communal being-in-the-world . . . the very existence, of the "we"' (Lash, 1994, p. 146) or communal being together (Maffesoli, 1996). This might reflect the future of distributed leadership, a leadership of being-in-the-world together and could reflect the need to develop leadership in context to draw leadership learning more towards the 'we' – communal being together.

These comments also seem to link once more to the recently developed notion of relational leadership (Cunliffe and Eriksen, 2011; Uhl-Bein, 2006), but advises a wider, more networked or distributed idea than that provided to date by this literature. Lash (1994), however, also points to the work of Habermas (1984) and suggests that the 'we' may not be based on shared meaning but on a chronic contest where speech acts are validity claims to be part of the 'we'. Interestingly, therefore, communities may not be built on shared meaning but on interactions of contest. Last, and to emphasize the notion of reflexive community further, Lash points to the work of Charles Taylor and his book on *Sources of Self*. Here Lash appears to indicate that Taylor's (1989) point is that we already have community and that what is important is where to look for it, and that this is where we need to connect into the aesthetic source of self through symbols and allegory. In conclusion, Lash suggests that communities are not about shared interests or shared properties but about shared meaning. He goes on to intimate that the fundamental sense of community should be 'worlded' and that reflexivity in the context of community must be 'in-the-world'. Herein, then, is a case for the study of leadership that is also reflexive and in-the-world. This could extend notions of 'worldly leadership', discussed at the beginning of this book, or at least provide a guiding principle for further research in the area, that aligns itself closely to context and shared meaning. This might well be better achieved through enthnographic and auto-ethnographic study. There also, though, needs to be the appreciation of reflexivity in accounts of leadership and a greater understanding of the dialectic (Collinson, 2005). Lash (1994) also points out the need to reflect on a 'mobile being-in-the-world' and 'diasporic' communities (communities into which we are thrown). These notions reflect the virtuality and fluidity of contemporary society and leadership researchers and theorists should also reflect on these issues for the postmodern interpretation of leadership.

IMAGINED COMMUNITY

Zygmunt Bauman (2001) looks at notions of community and reflects upon ideas of the aesthetic community. He introduces his book by specifying that words have meaning and feeling. Here he suggests that community is a word with feeling, as he denotes it feels good to 'have' or 'be in' a community. Community, he goes on to point out, 'is always a good thing' (Bauman, 2001, p. 1). These suggestions around community feeling are reminiscent of discussion of leadership and the positive regard to which this concept has been subjected (Collinson, 2012). Bauman goes on to describe why community feels good and he implies that this is owing to the warm feeling of which it holds promise. Community is a safe, cosy and comfortable place, a foundation to which Bauman returns to a number of times in his book: the place of security. Leadership can be said to be similarly described as a place of security, reducing anxiety (for example, Grint, 2010b) and hence providing safety. Similar to the discussion of Berry (1987) by Corlett (1989), discussed above, Bauman highlights the romanticized nature of community whereby inhabitants of a community might count on the good will of others in the same community to help each other in times of need. In his book, Bauman pops this bubble of romanticism as he points to the liquid modern world and suggests that this form of community is unattainable, and that it is always in the future a 'paradise lost . . . to which we dearly hope to return, and so we feverishly seek roads that may bring us there' (Bauman,

2001, p. 3). Leadership, as a notion, seems to suffer the same fate as an ideal to provide safety and security, yet it too is unattainable, always becoming (for example, Kempster and Stewart, 2010) and always in the future. We still seek it out, as Bauman describes the seeking of community, and it is this seeking that is at present an under-researched area of leadership studies. We, as leadership academics, research followership (for example, Hollander, 1995; Riggio et al., 2008; Shamir et al., 2007) but rarely do we entertain the idea of seeking and what it is that one seeks from or in 'leadership'.

Conversely, this may be what we have been researching all this while: our own needs of leadership, what it is that we as pockets of society, expect to see and feel. For instance, transformational leadership is a well-researched concept but reflects more the need of society rather than particular needs of followers or a 'holy grail' to leading. Bauman goes on to describe the postmodern world view of community-hostile reality. This reality, however, does not detract from us seeking the 'imagined community' that is warm and cosy, but sours on the imagination to seek community out and transcends into a difference between 'imagined community' and 'really existing community'. Again a parallel might be made here to leadership whereby recent critical notions problematize impressions of leadership (for example, Ford, 2010), yet this predictably will only lead to the intensified allure of the concept, if we are to take Bauman's point.

Additionally, Bauman makes an interesting observation of community when he shows that community, owing to the nature of shared understanding of a natural and tacit kind, can only be numb – or dead. He goes on to state:

> Once it starts to praise its unique valour, wax lyrical about its pristine beauty and stick on nearby fences wordy manifestoes calling its members to appreciate its wonders and telling others to admire them or shut up – one can be sure that the community is no more.
>
> (Bauman, 2001, pp. 11–12)

Here Bauman gives a stark commentary on what is evident in the leadership literature whereby the overly positive discourse concerning differing types of leadership, whether it is charismatic or ethical, transformational or authentic, is lauded at the same time as it falls from grace. This also presents an interesting dilemma to the leadership researcher – what happens when we question society about leadership and are given answers to what leadership is for those around us? To what extent are we then dismantling the concept for those who have initially constructed it? And does it then lose meaning? To what extent do we as leadership researchers walk away and leave the space we entered without leadership? Do we take this phenomenon away with us, back to the 'lab'? Do we create leadership by naming it so? These are questions we might ponder in our role as scholars of leadership and suggest a need to be reflexive and longitudinal in our approaches to studying leadership.

PEG COMMUNITIES, AESTHETIC COMMUNITIES AND IDOLS

Bauman continues by describing how when community collapses, identity becomes the 'the talk of the town' (2001, p. 15) and becomes a surrogate of community:

> Identity sprouts on the graveyard of communities, but flourishes thanks to the promise of a resurrection of the dead.
>
> (Bauman, 2001, p. 16)

From this Bauman describes the search for identity and that identity means standing out, being different. This again could act as a metaphor for individualistic notions of leadership, standing out and being different. However, Bauman goes on to describe how identity builders:

> . . . seek pegs on which they can hang their individually experienced fears and anxieties, and having done that, perform the exorcism rites in the company of other similarly afraid and anxious individuals . . . a respite from loneliness.
>
> (Bauman, 2001, p. 16)

These 'peg communities' are reflective of the contemporary postmodern world and could reflect ideas of distributed and networked notions of leadership (Balkundi and Kilduff, 2006) as peg communities to which multiple identities of leadership are formed, reassured and reformed.

Bauman goes on to highlight that the:

> . . . construction of identity is a never-ending and forever incomplete process, and must remain such to deliver on its promise . . . a truly until further notice kind of identity.
>
> (Bauman, 2001, p. 64)

He links this to views of the aesthetic community (Kant, 1790), where identity, like beauty, is based on shared agreement. Bauman points out that this is reflective of a postmodern community whereby members are promised 'a community of non-belonging, a togetherness of loners' (2001, p. 68). The postmodern search for idols (Klima, 1999) and individually fighting for identity, doing this all alone paradoxically makes the postmodern individual part of a community. As Bauman points out, Klima stresses that in the contemporary world individuals appear to need idols for security, permanence and stability in the world and Bauman goes on to suggest that this conjures up an 'experience of community' without real community, 'the joy of belonging without the discomfort of being bound' (Bauman, 2001, p. 69). These idols therefore, in leadership terms, keep the individual leader alive in contemporary society, and these 'leaders' serve a purpose of providing an experience of community. Bauman concludes that:

> The trick which idol-focused aesthetic communities accomplish is to transform community from a feared adversary of individual freedom of choice into a manifestation and reconfirmation of individual autonomy.
> (Bauman, 2001, p. 70)

Bauman, however, also highlights that aesthetic communities are not always centred on an idol but on threats, one-off events such as festivals, football matches or fashion. Bauman describes these as carnival bonds and 'carnival communities' where experience is to be on the spot and not to be taken home and consumed in the humdrum routine of daily life. Aesthetic communities can also be formed around problems and can be described as 'peg communities', and as Bauman points out, aesthetic communities do not reflect on ethical responsibilities and are 'bonds without consequences' (2001, p. 71). In leadership terms, we reflect on the idols and forget about the events and problems that create communities and the lack of reflection on ethics. Again, we might reflect on the issues on concentrating too much on the individual in leadership studies, which blind us to the contextual and background events that also link to the emergence and sustaining of leadership. This is where Bauman takes us next, the issue of ethics, and this book takes a look at these ideas in Chapter 7.

SUMMARY

This chapter has explored leadership from an art and aesthetic interpretation, as a symbolic construction within communities and how
this holds meaning for those within communities. The chapter points
to a number of alternatives when viewing leadership as a symbolic
construction. It could, for instance, be seen as a boundary construct
whereby it contributes towards marking out differences between
communities. It could also be seen as a ritual within groups that
serves as a fantasy of normalizing the group, organization or community. Last, it could be seen as an aesthetic frill that is seen working
on the boundary while also representing group norms. In addition,
the chapter has reviewed ideas of reflexive and imagined community
that remind us of the contextual, relational and ethical nature of
leadership as it is constructed within groups, organizations and communities. Whichever frame one uses, leadership from a relational
and symbolic standpoint seems to be spatially constructed providing
sense and meaning within and between groups and communities.

5. Leadership, liminality and social drama

There is a motel in the heart of every man. Where the highway begins to dominate the landscape, beyond the limits of a large and reduplicating city, near a major point of arrival and departure: this is most likely where it stands . . . One hundred hermetic rooms . . . Repeated endlessly on the way to your room, you can easily forget who you are; you sit on your bed and become man sitting on bed, an abstraction to compete with infinity itself; out of such places and moments does modern chaos raise itself to the level of mathematics. Despite its great size, the motel seems temporary. This feeling may rise simply from the knowledge that no one lives here for more than one or two days at a time.

(DeLillo, *Americana*, 1971, p. 257)

The quote above introduces and illustrates well the concept of liminality, which has also been described by Kamau (2002, p. 18) as episodes when:

. . . boundaries become fluid and identity becomes ambiguous. Normal regulations fall aside and life becomes dangerous, unpredictable, super-charged and exciting.

Although this description is slightly hyperbolic, it does appear to capture the essence of liminality in terms of fluidity and identity. Kamau goes on to describe liminality as being a borderline condition occurring on the boundaries, in the interstices and underneath society, where 'individuals lose their old statuses and identities' (2002, p. 19). The concept of liminality helps us to investigate the space between communities and hence enables us to reflect on leadership betwixt and between. And as Renfro-Sargent (2002, p. 83) observes, 'Borderlands are places of transition' so the link with leadership and issues of change become evident once more. Refro-Sargent also highlights the fluid nature of boundaries in society, implying that people are constantly in motion – a key feature of contemporary society. It is not surprising, therefore, that the concept of liminality is growing in the organization and management literature, being linked to consulting (Czarniawska and Mazza, 2003; Sturdy et al., 2006), identity (Beech, 2011), MBA study (Simpson et al., 2010), temporary workers (Garsten, 1999), individual and organizational learning (Tempest and Starkey, 2004) and leadership and leadership learning (Hawkins and Edwards, in press; Yip and Raelin, 2012).

In their paper, Hawkins and Edwards (forthcoming) stress the background to the concept of liminality. They point towards Turner (1979, 1987) seeing the concept as a state of between-ness and applying to individuals on the verge of a different stage of being. They also point towards the origins of liminality being in the anthropological study of tribal rituals, such as carnivals, pilgrimages, rites of passage or rituals in which the normative assumptions, relationships and conventional practices are suspended, hence drawing a link to community. By ritual Turner (1967) means a prescribed behaviour for occasions that has allusion to beliefs in mystical beings or powers. This point links back to the idea of leadership as ritual, first highlighted in the discussion around leadership, symbolism and art in the previous chapter. From Turner's description one could quite easily see charismatic leadership (for example, Conger and Kanungo, 1987, 1998) or similar ideas of romanticized leadership (Meindl, 1995; Meindl et al., 1985) as being a belief in mystical beings or power. Such a view becomes particularly pertinent if we take Weber's (1947) conception of charisma as literal and being centred on a special gift or divine origin. Other authors also seem to pick up on the link between liminality and charisma (for example, Andelson, 2002; Kamau, 2002). Kamau, for example, notes that like liminality, charismatic movements can be seen to be anarchic, disruptive and even dangerous, challenging and even rejecting normal society. Looking into notions of liminality, therefore, may provide a deeper understanding of the ritualistic nature of leadership based on symbolism and ideas of charisma.

LIMINALITY AND LEADERSHIP LEARNING

Hawkins and Edwards go on to propose that liminal moments have been described as moments in and out of time during which a transition occurs, transporting an individual from one state of being to another (Delanty, 2003 [2010]; Turner, 1969; Van Gennep, 1908 [1960]). Hawkins and Edwards use the example of a marriage ceremony as a liminal ritual within a Western culture that marks the transition from a single life to a new, shared life together. Liminality has also been used by anthropologists to examine the implications and function of rites and rituals for tribal cultures and those who inhabit them. It is seen by scholars such as Victor Turner as a period of reflection, 'a fruitful darkness' (1967, p. 110), a place of primitive hypothesis, 'where there is certain freedom to juggle with the factors of existence' (1967, p. 106). When looking at liminality in this way, it is easy to see the link that is made with leadership learning (Hawkins and Edwards, forthcoming). In leadership learning and development terms, reflection in spaces of change appears to be *the* area of deep learning regarding leadership (for example, Bennis and Thomas, 2002; Edwards et al., 2002). And, as Kamau (2002, p. 19) further elaborates,

> In liminal contexts, the constraints of ordinary lives have been removed. The individual no longer needs to wear a mask. Having been liberated from the constrictions of normal society, a person can be free to express his or her personal interests, preferences, and abilities. Participants are free to be 'authentic' – to be 'themselves'.

Kamau recommends that one must move outside society in order to be an authentic person owing to the artificial nature of constructed society. While this seems idealistic, there are connotations towards residential programmes of leadership development that I have experienced as a researcher, delegate and facilitator, where the emphasis is to learn through experiences of liminality (see Edwards et al., 2002). A safe environment, for example, is created for managers to experiment with certain styles, behaviours and attitudes, sometimes in challenging circumstances that are novel and strange. Also, the link to moving outside of society to be authentic, as advocated by Kamau, appears to have implications for notions of authentic leadership (for example, Avolio et al., 2004; George, 2003; Luthans and Avolio, 2003), as this would suggest that leaders, as they are engaged within society mechanisms, cannot be truly authentic. A point highlighted already in Chapter 3. Liminality, therefore, does not just seem important for leadership learning but also for developing specifically ideals of the authentic leader. It is questionable, however, the level to which literature and research on authentic leadership takes into account sociological ideas such as liminality.

Additionally, though, it must be highlighted that Kamau's comments are set within the context of 'intentional communities', those set up on purpose to sit outside mainstream society and hence this stands as an argument in favour of developing intentional communities. Whether this relates to more emergent communities in society is mute. Yet, one could also argue that organizations are in themselves intentional communities. Consequently, we sit back at the start of this discussion questioning the worth of concepts and notions of authentic leadership, especially given previous writing earlier in this book around leadership as character and caricature, symbolism, ritual and masks. All pertains towards a liminal episode or a less than authentic self. Maybe the best leadership learning can achieve is to enable leaders to cope with the mask, character and caricatures that they will need to wrestle with within their own context – time, place and space (discussed further below).

A similar but alternative view to that of Kamau (2002) is provided courtesy of Foster (2002), where he goes back to Turner (1969) and uses a quote by him to illustrate the ceremonial nature of liminality. Turner (1969, p. 82) describes the following,

> It is as though they are being reduced or ground down to a uniform condition to be fashioned anew and endowed with additional powers to enable them to cope with their new station in life.

I wonder to what extent leadership learning and development programmes are seen to be conducting such a process. Programmes developed in the 1960s and 1970s were, to my knowledge, linked to this idea of 'reducing down' to 'build back up'. Foster (2002, p. 70) goes on to describe an outcome of this process as 'intense egalitarianism and a sense of emotional unity'. This again relates to the discourse of 'life-changing' emotional reactions to some leadership development experiences that I have experienced as a facilitator of leadership learning. The concept of liminality, therefore, appears to hold important clues as to what it is that organizations do in the pursuit of developing leadership learning. They create intentional liminality as a safe space for learning. If this is the case it is worth looking more deeply into the liminal process.

THE LIMINAL PROCESS

Van Gennep (1908 [1960]) highlights three phases of undertaking a liminal ritual experience, which are 'Separation', '*Limen*' and 'Reincorporation'. According to the translators of his work, Solon Kimball and Monika Vizedom, Van Gennep sees regeneration as a law of life and advises the aforementioned three phases as typifying these changes in social life. The first phase, Separation, is where individuals are symbolically (and occasionally, for the purposes of the ritual, physically) detached from their previous role in the social structure and from related social ties and conventions. As Hawkins and Edwards (forthcoming) point out, this phase of 'Separation' also has an association with leadership, where leaders have often been framed at a distance (physical, symbolic or virtual) or as a 'heroic' character (Grint, 2010b). Grint goes on to describe leadership as sacred, separated in some way from followers. We see this form of separation linked to the notion of liminality. Indeed, Van Gennep (1908 [1960]) reminds us that sacredness is not an absolute but brought into play by situational variance. This reflects Grint's (2005a) notion of leadership constructed in response to 'wicked' problems, whereas management is constructed in response to 'tame' problems. This link to differing situations of change could provide a sense of the sacred to leadership.

The second phase is *Limen* or threshold, a state of transition that Turner (1967, p. 80) describes as 'a cultural realm that has few of the attributes of the previous or coming state', in which the liminal subject is 'passenger'. The third phase, Reincorporation, in which the transition is consummated, often ceremoniously, and the subject regains a stable, usually higher status identity with clearly defined roles and obligations in relation to others, and is once again expected to behave in line with culturally defined norms and ethical frameworks.

Further to the view of leadership as sacred, Van Gennep sees changes in a person's life as involving actions and reactions between sacred and profane. He goes on to describe, through the translators' words, that these 'actions and reactions are to be regulated and guarded so that society as a whole will suffer no discomfort or injury' (Van Gennep, 1908 [1960], p. 3). Here leadership may be the symbolic behaviour or the constructed notion that helps society guard against discomfort or injury. Leadership could be what

Adolf Bastien (1881) describes as a *Völkergedanken* or a 'folk idea', which ties with the writing of Van Gennep, at least according to the translators of his work.

Turner (1967, p. 102) highlights *'Sacra'* as being at the heart of the liminal matter. He indicates that there are three main components of *Sacra*:

1. Exhibitions – 'what is shown' – would include evocative arte-facts such as relics of deities, heroes or ancestors, such as musical instruments, masks, figurines and effigies.
2. Actions – 'what is done'.
3. Instructions – 'what is said'.

Largely, in leadership studies, aspect (2) tends to be well researched, further research needs to be developed about 'exhibitions' of leader-ship and 'what is said' as leadership, or the narrative of leadership. This latter point is discussed further in Chapter 7 where a discourse perspective on community is emphasized. Having said this, there is recent work looking at the narrative of leadership (for example, Mead, 2014). For now, however, the chapter turns towards related concepts of time, space and place to help make further sense of issues of liminality.

TIME, PLACE AND SPACE

> When refugees and community members move from one state of exist-ence to another, they are moving their cultures. Their way of life begins to change with the first step, and with it their identity begins to shift, redefined by space and place. Old identities dissolve and new identities are formed in the borderlands, and this process of identity change can be sought after or forced upon those who enter the liminal state.
>
> (Renfro-Sargent, 2002, pp. 90–1)

This quote exemplifies the transitional nature of liminality, as already discussed above. In this section it is the link it has to time, space and place. The quote also illustrates the permeable nature of identity and culture and suggests that the transition of identity and culture are bound by time, place and space. For instance, Renfro-Sargent (2002) highlights a case example from Palestine through the work of Peteet (1995), where she states:

Place, or village, in the Palestinian consciousness is what ties a person to the space of Palestine, Palestinians identify and refer to one another in terms of village of region of origin.

(Peteet, 1995, p. 170)

There are also links to the community literature here, where processes of culture based on understanding aspects such as those discussed in this book – learned, shared and symbolic – are integrated into a pattern that are distinct by virtue of time, space and the passage of events (Love Brown, 2002). What I believe Love Brown to be hinting towards is that what makes community rounded as a concept is an integration with context aspects of time and space. From this, therefore, one can conclude that any research into leadership should also look into aspects of time and space and frame the identity of 'leader' as fluid based on time, space and place. These crucibles of time, place and space are where there is the 'quest for identity, its loss, its resurrection and its reconstruction' (Renfro-Sargent, 2002, p. 103).

There are links here to the work of Dian Marie Hosking (1988, 2007) around processes of leadership, indeed there have also been recent calls for the development of more processual and communicative views of leadership (Tourish, 2013, 2014). These frames of processual leadership may be developed further by reflection and empirical investigation on time, space and place and how they relate to society (Low and Lawrence-Zúñiga, 2003). As Urban has stated, 'Physcial space is the medium through which culture travels' (1996, p. 66). Place also appears to offer a unique setting for leadership (Collinge et al., 2011). Collinge and colleagues have investigated the role of leadership in place making and place shaping. Within this investigation Collinge and Gibney (2011) draw on Cresswell's (2004) work to see place as a way of understanding the world. They also draw on the work of Massey (1993, 2005) to highlight the event of place, which they describe as a coming together of previously unrelated processes to form a constellation that is open and internally multiple and that stresses a level of fluidity. By taking place as a frame of reference Collinge and Gibney (2011) challenge the traditional frame of organizational leadership to see leadership as a wider social phenomenon, similar to the emphasis of this book. They go on to insinuate, similar to conclusions being drawn from this book, that leadership in this sense of place is underpinned by more cross-boundary or networked relational foundations. The conclusions drawn from this investigation into leadership and place are discussed by Mabey and Freeman (2011) whereby they empha- size a multi-perspective conceptual framework of linking leadership and place. As part of this framework they underline the importance of narratives, myths and stories in the articulation of place and the importance of capturing physical, mental and social elements of the production of space. They also suggest that place and space cannot be orchestrated by a single leader or leadership team. In relation to this suggestion by Mabey and Freeman, therefore, it seems a community perspective is useful in developing an understanding of leadership, as this may be where place and space are orchestrated. Community, therefore, is leadership.

If leadership studies are to lend themselves more to an ethno- graphic standpoint as some writers (for example, Edwards, 2011) suggest, then they must take account of issues of space. Urban stresses this, stating that space is central to the ethnographer. He also points towards narrative analysis as a particular way to understand issues of culture and space. Narrative and space therefore seem key to developing leadership studies research further and to respond to issues of contextualization (for example, Jepson, 2009; Osborn and Marion, 2009; Osborn et al., 2002; Porter and McLaughlin, 2006). Also, Urban advises an inherent fluidity to narrative and hence com- munity. He points to departures and arrivals as holding narrative together, just as comings and goings hold community together. He states, Time and again, departures threaten community, but arrivals rebuild it' (1996, p. 155). Herein lies an important notion for the study of leadership whereby there is fluidity in context and that on a basic level leaders will come and go and new leaders will be initiated into a space. At a deeper level, however, perceptions of leadership will come and go in context and the challenge for leadership scholars is to track this arrival and departure, this coming and going to gain a fluid interpretation of leadership in time, space and place. As Ropo and colleagues imply, 'places and spaces construct and perform leadership' (2013, p. 379).

In addition to ideas of time, space and place it appears that ideas around social drama – a linked notion to liminality discussed by Turner (1974) – may help to further develop ideas of leadership. The chapter now turns towards this concept to develop ideas of liminality and leadership.

LEADERSHIP WITHIN SOCIAL DRAMA

In anthropological terms, crisis is seen as an important factor in the disturbance of individuals and groups (Chapple and Coon, 1942, cited in the introduction to Van Gennep, 1960 by Solon Kimball). Kimball goes on to describe how Van Gennep sees crisis and disturbance within social settings as important in changing the status of individuals. This is similar to how charismatic leadership has been linked to social crisis in the past (Yukl, 2010). In his writing on anthropology, Van Gennep seems to see critical problems of becoming as important in social life, such as becoming male, becoming female and becoming old. The main translator of Ven Gennep's (1960) work, Kimball, makes an interesting point suggesting that these rituals of becoming have become too individualistic and can only be discovered in the 'privacy of the psychoanalyst's couch' (p. xvii). This is a statement from 1960 and appears to relate distinctly to issues discussed already in this book, one of the individualization of concepts of leadership. Instead, leadership should be seen as a process of becoming, similar to ideas expressed by Kempster and Stewart (2010), linked to critical problems that are played out in ritual processes in society. Herein, therefore, is a further call for a symbolic and cultural understanding of what leader becoming means in a context.

Related to notions about crisis, the literature on liminality also discusses a further concept, that of social drama (Turner, 1974). Turner sees social drama as a processual view of society and that these dramas arise in conflict situations. He indicates that they have four phases:

1. Breach – a symbolic trigger of confrontation or encounter occurs that breaches regular norm-governed social relations.
2. Crisis – this is where, if not sealed off quickly, the breach widens. This can be seen as the liminal stage of the social drama.
3. Redressive Action – Turner describes here that in order for the crisis to be limited certain adjustive and redressive mechanisms are brought into operation. These, he says, can be informal or formal, institutionalized or ad hoc.
4. Reintegration or Legitimization – this phase either ends in reintegration or the legitimization of the irreparable schism.

De Wolfe (2002) uses Turner's idea of social drama to analyse group activity in a particular context. From this analysis she evidences sub-groups and sub-social dramas that do not appear to be regarded by Turner in his conceptualization and that the breach that Turner describes as starting the social drama is ever-present.

Reflecting on the concept of social drama helps bring differing concepts highlighted in this book together. For example, it enables the character or caricature of leadership to be addressed within the drama, costume becomes an important aspect of the appearance of leadership and the backdrop, the place and space within which leadership is constructed becomes more visible to those researching leadership. Drawing these aspects together suggests leadership may be a ritual behaviour (Van Gennep, 1908 [1960]) that is replayed within social dramas and drawn from cultural myths and stories. We are able to see transition periods and subsequently issues of liminality can also be seen and addressed. Taking a community perspective, therefore, inherently advocates a dramaturgical methodology for studying leadership similar to that proposed by Hatch et al. (2005). Also, studying leadership in organizations, which may not necessarily be communities, could also use the concept of social drama. Seeing the organization as a social drama enables the understanding of character construction for leadership.

SUMMARY

This chapter has reviewed the literature on liminality and related it to the study of leadership. Liminality represents community as the in-between space. By conducting this review of liminality the chapter has highlighted the importance of space, place, time and social drama in ideas of community and hence in the study of leadership. The chapter also reiterates the importance of using methodologies such as taking ethnographic, anthropological and dramaturgical views when researching leadership. This will enable the researcher to gain a deeper appreciation of these connecting factors. The final two sections of this chapter underline an important link between leadership and ideas of ethics, language and a postmodern perspective. These are the main areas of reflection in the concluding two chapters.

6. Language, ethics and leadership

> Ethics begins only when the good is revealed to consist in nothing other than a grasping of evil and when the authentic and the proper have no other content than the inauthentic and the improper.
> (Agamben, 1993, p. 12)

> . . . what drives the nations of the earth toward a single common destiny is the alienation from linguistic being, the uprooting of all peoples from their vital dwelling in language.
> (Agamben, 1993, p. 82)

This chapter looks at the construction of leadership through an aspect of community – language. The link that this has with ethical notions of leadership is also reviewed and a discussion is held on the dualistic nature of ethics in leadership. Agamben's words above, therefore, seem to resonate with this chapter as he appears to be suggesting that we can only judge what is good in comparison to what is bad and vice versa, we can only judge what is bad in comparison to what is good. He goes on to put forward that good and evil have the same state of things, 'they are perfectly identical' (Agamben, 1993, p. 91). This relational sense of ethics and authenticity seems to connect well to the discussions held in this chapter where ideas of community that are based on a communicative view are explored.

In addition, the second quote from Agamben reflects the later discussion on the importance of language to community and hence to leadership and the current critique that leadership studies is taking a geographically defined nation-based perspective as opposed to an indigenous and community perspective and that language is lost (Edwards, forthcoming).

Discussing language in relation to leadership resonates ideas of ethicality and morality as language concerns the communicative nature of community. Delanty (2003 [2010]) suggests that community can be viewed as communicative in the sense of being formed in collective action based on place (discussed previously in Chapter 5). In this sense, he advocates communities are important vehicles for the recovery and expression of moral recognition. Therefore ideas of community as communicative appear to revolve around ideas of morals and ethics, similar to Maffesoli's (1996) observations from the literature that suggest ethical rules emerge from collectivities (Shields, 1996) and that consequently ethics is the glue that holds together the diverse elements of a given whole. The idea of community as communicative, however, also suggests the importance of communication and in particular for differing community-based languages and dialects. Ethics and language then form the basis for discussion in this chapter. The chapter also serves to bring concepts discussed in this book together and there is an attempt to explore the interrelational nature of the concepts explored so far. So, for instance, there is an attempt to turn back to ideas discussed in previous chapters (for example, symbolism, friendship, multiple belonging and liminality) and relate them to ideas of ethics, language and leadership discussed in this chapter. This inter-related nature is expressed through the work of Alasdair MacIntyre and his book *After Virtue* (1984 [1991]) as this work provides a useful commentary on ethics and ethicality and a basis upon which leadership can be reflected.

COMMUNITY, ETHICS AND LEADERSHIP

The link between ethics and community is not necessarily a new avenue for theoretical or empirical consideration. Etzioni (1993), for example, suggests that the communitarian view is to call for the restoration of civic virtues and to shore up the moral foundations of society. Indeed, Etzioni's view of community appears to be inherently ethical and virtuous. He offers that the communities in which we grow and develop are the basis for our development of values and that the communities of which we are a part then go on to be important in sustaining our moral voices in addition to our inner self. Etzioni's views are very forthright to the extent that his book – *The Spirit of Community* – is openly a manifesto for a communitarian society and therefore needs to be treated with critical judgement.

The link, though, between ethics and community also appears elsewhere. Donaldson and Dunfee (1994), for instance, have developed a framework based on integrative and social contracts theory (ISCT) that attempts to blend community-based perspectives of ethics and universal norms (Cunha et al., 2010). The model suggests that a norm would be (1) created within a given community; (2) generally accepted by the members of that community; (3) abided by the majority of the members of that community; (4) in line with universal indisputable ethical principles; and (5) subject to prioritization by rules previously agreed upon. Cunha et al. (2010), however, criticize this model for being functionalist in nature and hence not adding much more than those models and theories highlighted above. Also, this chapter stresses the lack of theoretical consideration of community and the differing perspectives and fluidity of concepts associated with community (Delanty, 2003 [2010]). This chapter, then, contributes further by exploring previously highlighted links between theories of community and ideas of leadership (Edwards, 2011, 2012).

Cunha et al. (2010) recommend that notions of ethics and leadership need to be developed along five motives: (1) avoid 'black and white' views of ethical leadership and appreciate the 'grey areas' (Bruhn, 2008) or 'twilight zones' (Nel et al., 1989) of ethics; (2) adopt a process/relational approach (for example, Bradbury and Lichtenstein, 2000) to ethical leadership; (3) avoid dispositional and situational deterministic explanations; (4) present ethical leadership as a social construction; and (5) incorporate the role of ambiguity in the process of ethical leadership (Cunha et al., 2010, p. 200).

Cunha and colleagues use the concept of liminality or being in *Limen,* discussed previously in Chapter 5, to explore these motives. As mentioned above, this chapter goes further and explores other aspects of community in relation to leadership and ethics as framed by MacIntyre's discussion in *After Virtue.*

AFTER VIRTUE: A WIDER PERSPECTIVE OF LEADERSHIP, ETHICS AND COMMUNITY

In *After Virtue* MacIntyre (1984 [1991]) reviews philosophical discussions of virtue that appear to develop from individualistic concepts towards those based on community ideals. From this initial observation, therefore, it seems important to consider the duality of individualism and community in understanding the ethics of leadership. For example, Knights and O'Leary (2006) point to the preoccupation with individualistic notions of leadership, especially in relation to contemporary business ideals, but fall short in recognizing the duality to which MacIntyre refers. Indeed, Delanty (2003 [2010]) advises that individualism is a core element in understanding community. MacIntyre recognizes this at various stages throughout *After Virtue*, not least through the recognition of Nietzsche's (1974) work (on page 114), but also in examples such as:

> Each of us, individually and as a member of particular social groups, seeks to embody his own plans and projects in the natural and social world.
> (MacIntyre, 1984 [1991], p. 104)

And when discussing 'The Heroic Society':

> Courage is important, not simply as a quality of individuals, but as the quality necessary to sustain a household and a community. Kudos, glory, belongs to the individual who excels in battle or in contest as a mark of recognition by his household and his community.
> (MacIntyre, 1984 [1991], p. 123)

It is the idea of community that holds the most promise for MacIntyre in trying to make sense of ethics, virtue and morals:

> . . . the moral protagonist stands in a relationship to his community and his social roles which is neither the same as that of the epic hero nor again the same as that of modern individualism.
> (MacIntyre, 1984 [1991], p. 143)

This discourse would advocate not just a community perspective but also a relational perspective, which is also developing in the leadership literature (for example, Cunliffe and Eriksen, 2011; Fairhurst, 2007). In addition, Isaacs (2011) takes a relational approach when discussing moral responsibility in collective contexts:

> . . . we need to start understanding ourselves in relation to others, as members of communities who can act together as moral agents.
> (Isaacs, 2011, p. 9)

It appears, therefore, that the ideas around relational leadership are important in making sense of leadership from a community perspective as they are intrinsically linked to ethics. For instance, while MacIntyre appears to recognize the relational angle, a criticism of his work is a lack of considering how community might be represented or theorized. This is an aspect to which this chapter responds and provides some understanding of community within conceptualizations of ethics and leadership. The chapter starts this discussion by connecting ideas of community through symbolism and ideas of 'character' developed by MacIntyre and discussed in detail previously in the book in Chapter 1.

SYMBOLISM AND THE 'CHARACTER' OF LEADERSHIP

Initially when reading MacIntyre (1984 [1991]), one gets an impression of a parallel discourse within ethics and leadership. For example, MacIntyre's comments regarding emotive theory resonate with some individualistic models of leadership, especially ethical (for example, Mendonca and Kanungo, 2007), charismatic (for example, Conger and Kanungo, 1987; House, 1977) and transformational (for example, Bass, 1985; Bass and Riggio, 2006) theories that emphasize the need for the 'leader' to manipulate people's views (and potential of what is 'right' and 'wrong') through emotive language. Indeed, MacIntyre goes on to indicate that:

> . . . emotivism informs a great deal of contemporary moral utterance and practice and more specifically that the central 'characters' of modern society – in the special sense which I assigned to the word 'character' – embody such emotivist modes in their behaviour.
>
> (MacIntyre, 1984 [1991], p. 73)

MacIntyre's 'characters' and how we associate with characters through, among other aspects of social life, drama (he uses Japanese Noh play and English medieval morality plays) appears to be an important consideration for ethics and leadership. MacIntyre advises that we engage with the character rather than the actor. Here, then, we might assume a performative sense of leadership (for example, Ford et al., 2008) whereby leadership and the ethics of leadership are built into a character format and we identify not with 'the leader' but with the character of leadership, which is culturally constructed. Similar to MacIntyre, where he describes the 'manager' as a character, we may represent the leader (or the ethical leader) in the same way. If so, just as MacIntyre describes the manager as character:

... the obliteration of the distinction between manipulative and non-manipulative social relations ... [and is] not able to engage in moral debate.

(MacIntyre, 1984 [1991], p. 30)

Maybe the 'character' of leader, despite the promise of inherent ethicality from theories such as transformational leadership (Bass and Steidlmeier, 1999), suffers the same fate. Or it is the way that leadership has been popularized as a concept with business (Ford and Harding, 2007) that has developed a certain character that is constructed as inherently moral.

These issues thus bring into question the very use of the leadership discourse in business organizations. Indeed, Grint (2005b) suggested that concepts of leadership derive from a military term and its use in other organizations is mute. As a result we might put forward that leadership as a concept or 'character' may not compute with the business environment, not least in the sense that it is discussed in moralistic terms within the popular leadership discourse (for example, Ciulla, 2004a, 2004b). Alternatively, the business sector may be developing its own 'character' of leadership that is based on a high bonus culture and an 'it's just business' attitude. It may be this character of leadership within business that needs to be dissected in terms of ethical leadership.

To develop the idea of 'character' further we might link it to ideas of community and, particularly, symbolic representation of community. Earlier in this book the idea of symbolic representation in relation to the leadership literature was highlighted whereby leadership is represented by symbolism of and from community. As featured in Chapter 1, here we might accentuate images of good and bad as metaphors (for example, Alvesson and Spicer, 2010), from religious forms of 'the saint' and 'the sinner' to the dualist concepts of 'the good deity' and 'the evil deity', to more contemporary comic book iconography of 'the hero' and 'the villain' (see Edwards et al., forthcoming a). This idea of leadership represented through symbolism appears to resonate with the idea of 'character' in that if one is to take a community perspective, then the character of leadership is represented through the symbolism within the community. Ethicality and the representation thereof of leadership are enacted through symbolic community representation. A form of community symbolism that is prominent and highly influential is language.

LANGUAGE, ETHICAL LINGUISTIC SURVIVAL AND THE IMPORTANCE OF 'TRADITION'

Habermas (1984) suggests that social action is based on language and that society is linguistically created. This emphasizes the importance of language research in leadership and how this language can be colonized or Anglo-sized through professional/business discourse (Jepson, 2009). Consequently, concepts or characters of leadership might be reflected in, or bounded by, common language, discourse and dialect (Edwards, 2012). Ethical judgements are developed through a shared narrative and it is important to investigate and appreciate who the participants are in this shared narrative. The recognition of what is or is not ethical leadership may be linguistically and symbolically created but, as highlighted above, is contextually bound. This resonates with discussion in the community view of leadership around symbolism and language. Indeed, MacIntyre has stated, 'moral judgements are linguistic survivals from the practices of classical theism which have lost the context provided by these practices' (1984 [1991], p. 60). With both symbolism and language there appears the need to understand ethics and leadership within context and tradition. Tradition is a prominent aspect of MacIntyre's work:

> A living tradition ... is an historically extended, socially embodied argument, and an argument precisely in part about the goods which constitute that tradition. Within a tradition the pursuit of goods extends through generations, sometimes through many generations. Hence the individual's search for his or her good is generally and characteristically conducted within context defined by those traditions of which the individual's life is a part, and this is true both of those goods which are internal to practices and of the goods of a single life.
>
> (MacIntyre, 1984 [1991], p. 222)

Hence, a tradition of ethics and leadership identified through symbolism and language appears important in understanding leadership in organizations. This will enable a deeper appreciation of what is seen as ethical within and across organizations that draws on a more historical context, an area advised as lacking in organization studies (for example, Clark and Rowlinson, 2004). This chapter now tries to draw together some of these ideas by using some perspectives from previous chapters – friendship, aesthetics and multiple belonging.

FRIENDSHIP, SOCIAL NETWORKS AND THE ETHICS OF LEADERSHIP

An interesting aspect stressed by MacIntyre is his recollection of the work of Moore in _Principa Ethica_ (1902) whereby MacIntyre suggests that the following was seen as the fundamental truth of moral philosophy:

> The achievement of friendship and the contemplation of what is beautiful in nature or in art become certainly almost the sole and perhaps the sole justifiable ends of all human action.
>
> (MacIntyre, 1984 [1991], p. 15)

Indeed, when discussing 'The Heroic Society', MacIntyre (1984 [1991], p. 123) talks of the importance of ideals of courage and fidelity and how they are entwined with impressions of friendship and loyalty. MacIntyre also underlines Aristotle's idea of friendship being a virtue in itself. Earlier in this book it was suggested that friendship (and/or betrayal) (for example, French, 2008; French ct al., 2009; Phal, 2000) and/or social networks (for example, Balkundi and Kilduff, 2006) might encourage a broader and less formal view of leadership not necessarily bounded by organizations but played out in society generally. This could help bring friendship more into organizational life and promote it from the relegation into private life highlighted by MacIntyre. Theoretical consideration around organizational leadership as a result needs to develop an understanding of what friendship means in differing cultures and communities and how this relates to the construction of what is and is not ethical. In addition, this would be a fruitful area of research in organizations that would enable us to explore the power dynamics of friendship and social networks as a source of leadership, especially given the growing influence social network tools such as Facebook and Twitter are having on working lives.

BEAUTY, ETHICS AND LEADERSHIP

In the quote from MacIntyre above he also discussed the aspect of what one considers as beautiful as a purpose of human action. Further to MacIntyre's reflections Shields (1996) also points towards the aesthetic and beauty in connection with the ethical. He notes that questions of beauty and correctness as defined by the collective experience are reflective of the classical notion of aesthetics. In this sense, he proposes that rather than looking for 'universal rights and wrongs one deals with questions of appropriateness and "fit" within situations' (Shields, 1996, p. xi). There is therefore a need to develop research along the lines of a perspective of beauty and what is seen as beautiful and aesthetically pleasing as ethical. Leadership that is seen, as beautiful, therefore, may be wrongly assumed to be ethical and vice versa leadership that is deemed ugly, may be wrongly assumed to be unethical. There is also an added complication here, as ugliness may be seen as beautiful, and beauty as ugly. This would be a fruitful area of research in addition to the aesthetic standpoint already evident in the leadership literature and discussed in chapter four. This avenue of research throws up a number of different questions, such as, like beauty, to what extent is leadership seen through the eye of the beholder? To what extent do we see leadership through attraction? This is an important question given the seemingly inherent positivity of the concept (Collinson, 2012). Do we then see leadership as positive because we see it as beautiful?

MULTIPLE BELONGING: ETHICALITY, MULTIPLE IDENTITIES AND LIMINAL SPACES

In MacIntyre's book he goes on to describe how individuals are identified as their roles (or characters, from the discussion held above) and it is these roles that bind individuals to communities, 'I confront this world as a member of this family, this household, this clan, this tribe, this city, this nation, this kingdom' (1984 [1991], p. 172). Just as symbolism may mark out the boundaries with regards to ethics and leadership of and within differing groups, a sense of belonging appears to give an understanding of the connectivity that underpins a shared identity. Ethics and leadership will be linked to a sense of belonging that individuals have towards various socioeconomic groups (that is, family, work, society, religious and so on) outside the traditional work organization. However, the critical point in a community perspective of leadership is an understanding of community in postmodern society (Agamben, 1993; Blanchot, 1988; Corlett, 1989; Maffesoli, 1996; Nancy, 1991), where group membership has become more porous and fluid (Bauman, 2000) – an age of multiple belongings (Delanty, 2003 [2010]). Indeed, leadership has been represented as having multiple identities (Ford et al., 2008), but not as being linked to multiple belongings. This needs further research and reflection. Similarly, MacIntyre draws on a multiple identity based on a classical tradition:

> ... man is to fill a set of roles each of which has its own point and purpose: member of a family, citizen, soldier, philosopher, servant of God. It is only when man is thought of as an individual prior to and apart from all roles that 'man' ceases to be a functional concept.
>
> (MacIntyre, 1984 [1991], p. 59)

An important additional concept that has been highlighted earlier is the idea of liminality (Turner, 1969; Van Gennep, 1908 [1960]). Turner (1960), for instance, argues that community needs to be understood in opposition to structure. Additionally, 'in-between' places that are beginning to have growing importance in people's lives – the airport lounge, the commuting train or shopping centres (Delanty, 2003 [2010]). Liminality therefore appears particularly important when considering the study of leadership in organizations or leadership between organizations and has been discussed already in the literature by Cunha et al. (2010) and described above.

SUMMARY

This chapter has concentrated largely on the work of Alasdair McIntyre and his book *After Virtue* as it helps to provide a connective insight into other chapters and themes in this book. For example, the chapter seems to have provided an adhesion between concepts already reviewed in the book, such as character, friendship, liminality and a sense of belonging. This adhesion assists in bringing the book together and provides a chance for further reflection on key conceptual components of community that have a bearing on the direction of leadership studies. Before this book concludes it is also worth reflecting on more postmodern interpretations of community and how these impact on leadership research and reflection.

7. The postmodern community and leadership

Leaders live in a centrifugal field, pulled in opposing directions
by the competing demands of novelty and continuity and by
those of the institutional and the personal.
(Krantz, 2006, p. 224)

While some postmodern perspectives have already been explored in the book, such as the reflexive community and the imagined community (see Chapter 4), there are still some postmodern ideas of community that merit further exploration in relation to the study of leadership. For example, postmodern interpretations of community (Agamben, 1993; Blanchot, 1988; Corlett, 1989; Maffesoli, 1996; Nancy, 1991) reflect group membership as fluid and porous – an age of multiple belongings (Delanty, 2003 [2010]). Researchers studying leadership, therefore, should be sympathetic to the idea of multiple belongings and hence be sympathetic to the idea of leadership being multiply distributed. The book has already highlighted this fluidity through notions of multiple belonging in Chapters 2 and 6. Within this chapter, however, a deeper exploration into postmodern perspectives is conducted and linked back to the study of leadership. Community in the postmodern age is seen as being constructed through discourse, media and shared meaning. Further reflections on these aspects of community in relation to leadership are also represented.

COMMUNITY, ANARCHY AND LIBERTY

Michael Taylor's work has been highlighted in the introduction to this book regarding core characteristics of community and the link between friendship and community. It is also worth noting, however, his more critical comments regarding anarchy and liberty and the connection of these social constructs to community. For example, he points out in his discussion that communities are not continuously harmonious places and that there are inherent tensions, constraints on individual action and places where individuals might be persuaded to do things they would not ordinarily do. Herein, Taylor reminds us of the more negative side of community that one might associate with control and even coercion and hence a lack of individual liberty. This is reminiscent of more critical writers on leadership that might see the construct of leadership as a further extension of this controlling mechanism within organizations and groups and that leadership, while being lauded as a conduit to individual liberty, is in fact diminishing individual freedom. It is more critical commentary such as this that helps develop a balanced view on community perceptions and hence a balanced view on concepts of leadership.

COMMUNITY AS DISCOURSE

> Social processes are intrinsically murky, unclear, mysterious. People encountering other people outside the warmth and security of their families is dangerous, unpredictable. Communal reality is mercurial and shifting, alliances and loyalties unstable; individuals whimsical and unfathomable. From the point of view of a circulating discourse, counting on social relations for its survival, communal reality is a nightmare.
>
> (Urban, 1996, p. 147)

An interesting frame for the conceptualization of community in the postmodern perspective comes from Urban (1996), where he suggests that discourse brings about a semblance of order from the ambiguity represented above by creating images of community. In his book *Metaphysical Community* he develops ideas of discourse and community that build on anthropological work he has carried out over his career, but particularly studies of an Amerindian community within the interior of Brazil. From these studies Urban highlights the significance of meaning and how meaning is circulated and shared and hence the importance of the vehicles of meaning. He recommends that discourse is the most central of these vehicles and that the discourse that achieves the widest currency is that which helps a community to exist in the world. Within this evaluation, however, he points out that the circulation and repetition of talk is more significant than talk itself in fashioning community, providing the glue through which communities are built. This is symbolic and aesthetic as well as through talk. Urban uses the example of body painting in indigenous culture, which in some instances is related to preserving the memory of ancestors. Not everyone paints the same symbols or designs as they are based on attributes of ancestors. But it is the circulating and repetition of discourse through talk and aesthetic that creates and sustains a community.

Discourse, for Urban, therefore sits at the centre of tension between intelligibility and sensibility and this tension should be incorporated into any theory of culture. Social organization, he suggests, is the medium by which discourse circulates and its physical movement takes place across space and time. He stresses that this occurs through repetition. Discourse and social organization thus have a dual relationship whereby each is important for the other.

Straight away there are important links to be made to leadership. The intangibility of leadership has a long history and its use and exploration of meaning does appear to be prominent in the literature and organizational talk. We can also see a rising interest in discursive studies of leadership as a fruitful area of research in contemporary leadership studies. By taking this standpoint, leadership, similar to community, could be an image created by discourse to calm the ambiguous and inherently political reality of social interaction outside one's direct family, as Urban highlights in the quote at the beginning of this section. Besides, as Urban points out, as images of community are built on discourse as well as embodied practices, each instance of image encoding is represented by a negotiation between discourse and practice. Hence, images of leadership could also be seen as a negotiation between discourse and embodied practice, leading to further confusion over the term 'leadership'.

Developing an understanding of community, and for that matter, leadership, from a discourse perspective lends itself to a critical understanding of the role of language, as emphasized by Urban. As he suggests, language is an important factor in the experience of an object or concept as meaningful. The discussion of language has been further developed in the previous chapter. Language, though, may not suffice and Urban advises that a sensory understanding is also needed to enable meanings to be recovered within community practice. Here he highlights the importance of the two working in tandem to develop a discourse perspective whereby meaning is built up from repeated encounters with discourse as a physical object, such as that in texts, artefacts and speech. Taking this viewpoint, he continues, ensures that the researcher is picking something up from the senses as well as from the observation. This retrieval of information from the senses appears to resonate with recent calls for the greater understanding of the embodiment of leadership (for example, Pullen and Vachhani, 2013), where the materiality and aesthetic of leadership are promoted in making sense of leadership in context.

One aspect that draws prominence in Urban's work is the importance of the dream narrative. This seems particularly important given the visionary nature of leadership, as has been promoted by some scholars (for example, Saskin, 1988). This also appears important given the storytelling nature of leadership (for example, Denning, 2004, 2005). From the Western paradigm dreams are not for public consumption; as Urban notes, we hear of the 'leader's waking thoughts about the world, but we never discuss his or her dreams' (1996, p. 9). Here one may contend this notion through the paradigm of visionary leadership that from an individualistic view, prescribes that leaders communicate their future visions (dreams?) of the world. However, what Urban describes is a more tangible link between what one dreams directly with communication within the community and it being an important vocalizing exercise in the wider group dynamic. Urban goes on to connect discourse and culture to ideas of space, an area discussed in Chapter 5. He suggests that discourse helps define culture by mapping social interactions onto physical space and hence symbolizing and making that space meaningful. Discourse, he points out, distinguishes between sensible and intelligible space and in so doing enables itself to be circulated.

Urban goes on to state, 'Discourse illuminates what can be plainly seen, enchanting perceptible space, making it more real than it is to the senses' (1996, p. 88). Discourse also seems to be useful in responding to the characterization and disembodiment of leadership, highlighted in Chapter 1. Spatial discourse, Urban proposes, is able to bridge the sensible and intelligible, moving back and forth between perception and knowledge. Going back to the discussion around character and caricature of leadership that, I have argued disembodies leadership, it could be the discourse angle that may help us to explore this discussion further. For example, it appears discourse may be able to uncover the characterization process, as Urban suggests, where role expectations reside in discourse rather than the behaviour described by discourse. Leadership studies, it would appear, have been relating to the behaviour or interaction described in discourse (for example, transformational and transactional leadership behaviours) rather than seeking out what is meaningful about roles and the expectations these carry from discourse itself. Some scholars, such as Larsson and Lundholm (2010), have started good work around this slightly different direction by investigating leadership derived from everyday work interactions. It seems this theme should be developed and continued in mainstream leadership research.

CULTURAL COMMUNITY

In addition, and in part, to his reflections on ideas of the reflexive community, Lash (1994) highlights the view of cultural community where he points out the work of Hall and Jefferson (1976) and Fiske and Hartley (1978) in the cultural studies literature. This literature points out the media interpretation of culture and that what is important is cultural consumption as opposed to cultural production. Based on this idea, therefore, communities might be seen not as shared meaning and experience but more as in classical economics with producers and consumers (Lash, 1994). This is a point I have emphasized previously when investigating leadership through the lens of historical anthropological studies of indigenous communities (Edwards, forthcoming). Culture, consequently, is packaged for the consumption of those interacting within and across certain communities, such as expatriates, similar to a package holiday excursion. This relates to leadership in the sense that leadership would also be a culturally embedded phenomenon produced for the consumption of organizational actors. Within this notion of cultural community the idea of sub-culture is also highlighted by Lash through the work of Hebdige (1979) and is related to the symbolic through ritual and ceremony. The ritual or ceremony confirms the group's view of itself through repetitive action and therefore comforting individuals in the group (Maffesoli, 1996). Maffesoli, however, links this to the idea of emotional community that I turn to now.

EMOTIONAL COMMUNITY

In his book *The Time of Tribes*, Michel Maffesoli suggests that being together is a given and explores the undirected being together

through the idea of the emotional community. He proposes that
this undirected being together transcends individualism through the
'dynamic rootedness' of an undefined mass, the faceless crowd and
the tribalism that consist of a patchwork of small local entities. He
attaches these ideas to a notion of the puissance of the masses to
reflect the fluidity of modernity and the role of community within
a postmodern interpretation. It takes ideas of the social network
further by providing an ethical, aesthetic and fluid interpretation
of how social groups interact. Leadership studies needs to grasp
these fluid ideas of modernity in reconciling or even problematizing
the perception of leadership in social settings. Ethnographic and
longitudinal approaches therefore seem to be the most appropriate
methodologies for uncovering this fluidity. Interestingly, Maffesoli
stresses a need in the emotional community to gather round a protective figure, what we as leadership scholars might call a leader. In
modern times, though, Maffesoli suggests that the religious patron
saint is replaced by a guru, celebrity or the football team. This marks
out the changing nature of the protective figure and in our case the
changing nature of the 'leader'. Maffesoli goes on to highlight the
symbolic nature of this leadership function (which also draws
together the discussions held in Chapter 4 around the symbolic and
the aesthetic). He implies that in modern times once the power of
the symbolic function has ceased or fractured, the equilibrium of the
leader-follower relationship is relinquished and the role of the leader
as guarantor no longer works.

Maffesoli uses Weber's (1978) original ideas to develop the
theme and feature the characteristics of the emotional community
as a changeable composition, ill-defined nature, local flavour and
their lack of organization and routinization. This instability in the
emotional community makes established ethical or moral order
difficult, yet it also means there is a lack of strict conformity among
its members, Maffesoli describes the emotional community being
driven by a 'law of the milieu' that is difficult to escape. He uses
examples such as the Mafia, the business world and the intellectual
realm and highlights the variability of the degree of belongingness.
This is important given previous discussion on belonging in Chapter
2. Herein we see variability in attachment as well as variability in the
drivers for belonging, an additional note to develop in the study of
leadership and sense of belonging.

THE COMMUNITY OF DESTINY

In one of the concluding chapters of his book *The Time of Tribes*, Maffesoli also discusses the concepts of proxemics and the 'genius of place' to imply the idea of the community of destiny. This seems to be a further exploration of his notion of being together within a given society. Here he draws on the idea of man in relation not just to other individuals but also to the landscape, the city, the environment shared with other individuals. He suggests that these are the day-to-day histories of a community and describes them as 'time crystallized in space'. In relation to leadership studies these ideas may help us to contextualize leadership not just in a relational sense but also in a spatial sense.

Moreover, Maffesoli discusses the 'genius of place' where he indicates that this assures the link between time and space and is the 'non-conscious' guardian of sociality and that space is a concentrated form of time. Here he draws on the love of the nearby and the present and suggests that it is a collective memory that creates the community of destiny. He concludes that the 'community of destiny is an accommodation to the natural and social environment, and as such is forced to confront heterogeneity in its various guises' (1996, p. 126). He goes on to propose that proxemics is the foundation of a succession of 'we's' that constitutes an essence of sociality. The tribes he argues for in modern society are interspersed spatiality and arise from a feeling of belonging and function on a specific ethic within a communication network. These are aspects of leadership from a collective and network viewpoint that need to be developed and researched further.

The basis of this research could be developed through looking back towards a sense of belonging (as discussed in Chapter 2) by investigating what Maffesoli calls 'rituals of belonging'. Leadership could be either seen as a ritual of belonging or as creating a notion of a ritual of belonging. As Maffesoli describes, the ritual – by reinforcing a sense of belonging – can play the role of aspiration or the future ideal and thus can be the glue that allows groups to exist. From this idea of a community of destiny, Maffesoli goes on to discuss ideas of a network of networks, which goes further in terms of understanding leadership in a larger, more complex and inter-related sense than existing notions of distributed, collective or network ideas of leadership. As Maffesoli describes:

> ... a space where everything is combined, multiplied and reduced,
> making kaleidoscopic figures with ever changing and varied contours.
>
> (Maffesoli, 1996, p. 147)

On the issue of a network of networks Maffesoli concludes:

> Participating in a multitude of tribes, which are themselves interrelated,
> allows each person to live his or her intrinsic plurality. These various
> 'masks' are ordered in a more or less conflictual way and fit together with
> other surrounding 'masks'.
>
> (Maffesoli, 1996, p. 147)

Here he suggests that we can now to some extent see the morphology
of the network and we need to refrain from seeing it as a static entity
to which we ascribe a linear notion of leadership. Herein, therefore,
we are able to see leadership in a networked sense more lucidly
within a fluid context, ever-shifting and evolving around notions
such as friendship, belonging and ethics. In the next section we take
another look at friendship and community, but again through a
postmodern lens.

THE UNAVOWABLE COMMUNITY

In his book, *The Unavowable Community*, Maurice Blanchot (1988)
draws on ideas of friendship, already discussed in Chapter 3 of this
book, and the links this has to ideas of community. In particular, he
draws on the possibility of community and elaborates that friendship is linked to this possibility of community. He also indicates that
death, disaster and absence allow for the possibility of community.
In this exploration Blanchot discusses the relations between exigency
and community and describes a time of having lost the ability to
understand community, an age of either denial of community or an
age of nostalgia for modes of being in community. He draws out
the plurality of others and the tendency towards a communion, yet
also highlights the finitude of community and the finitude of those
beings that form a community. On the purpose of community,
Blanchot seems to suggest that it is a concept of sharing something,
much larger than just being together. Herein Blanchot proposes that
we need to understand being as part of sharing through speech and
silence. He also takes inspiration from Jean-Luc Nancy and features

the importance of the literary community and the power of the symbolic through writing. Also, he draws out the ultimate act of sharing as a community through birth and death. Here he draws on Nancy (discussed further below) again and emphasizes death as *the* true community, the impossible communion and suggests that community is revealed by the death of the other person. Linked to death is birth, the other extreme, and here Blanchot has similar views to Nancy, who says, 'we never stop being born into community' (Nancy, 1991, p. 66).

In addition, and of interest for a leadership perspective, Blanchot intimates that community is not the place of sovereignty. He goes on to say that the absence of community is not a failure of community but is part of community as absence belongs to community in the form of an extreme moment. Last, Blanchot is influenced heavily by the writing of Georges Bataille and talks of community in two facets – a public community and a secret community. Blanchot uses Bataille's ideas in drawing out the idea of the negative community – the community of those who have no community. The interchange between the possibility and impossibility of community as well as the negative community marks out the notion of the unavowable community. A similar view is held by Nancy and his ideas of the inoperative community. Before explicit links are made to leadership, this concept is reviewed next.

THE INOPERATIVE COMMUNITY

In a similar vein to that of Blanchot, Nancy's book, *The Inoperative Community* (1991), explores a postmodern outlook of community based on ideas of ecstasy, death, love and myth. He draws particularly on the work of Martin Heidegger, Georges Bataille, Karl Marx, Rousseau, as well as Maurice Blanchot (among other writers and philosophers). By doing so he provides a multi-perspective portrait of community that draws out the desire for community, the threshold of community, the external limits of community and ultimately the point, meaning and movement of community. Nancy suggests that 'community is what we are being called toward, or sent to, as our own most future' (1991, p. 71).

Similar to Blanchot, Nancy sees political space as the site of community and a measure of community as being-in-common, as Conner (1991), a commentator on Nancy's work, goes on to imply;

it is the existence of being-in-common and hence the existence of being-self. Conner goes on to explain this further and suggests that being-in-common is nothing to do with communion but rather to no longer having a substantial identity and the sharing of this 'lack of identity'. Here Conner explains the notion of finitude, the central concept in both Blanchot's and Nancy's interpretation of community. As Conner states, 'finitude, or the lack of infinite identity . . . is what makes community' (1991, p. xxxviii). Nancy sees the individual as a residue from the experience of the dissolution of community, an atom or the indivisible.

In addition, another commentator on Nancy's work – Christopher Fynsk – points out that Nancy links the experience of community to the experience of freedom and ultimately the experience of the real and the opening of time and space. Here Nancy draws explicitly on Bataille and talks of the inner experiences and that community is a space itself that enables an experiencing of the outside or of the outside-of-self. Nancy goes on to state, 'community is the ecstatic consciousness of the night of immanence . . .' (1991, p. 19). Like Blanchot, Nancy introduces the notion of finitude through the concepts of love and death. According to Nancy, community is calibrated by death and community reveals itself in the death of others. Community, he says, takes place through others and for others and that a community is the presentation to its members of their mortal truth. Love, on the other hand, Nancy insinuates is the extreme limit of community, lovers he says are poised at the extremity of sharing, meaning that they are both outside and inside community.

Nancy also links community to language and, as Fynsk (1991) points out, Nancy defines community as the limits of language and even the origin of language. Fynsk, in the foreword to *The Inoperative Community*, goes on to suggest that Nancy sees the political as implying experience of community as communication. Nancy implies the literary community, as does Blanchot, through writing. It is writing, Fynsk proposes, that enables a community to enjoin its own dissemination and further suggests that this constitutes the law of community. As Nancy argues, 'Each writer, each work inaugurates community' (1991, p. 68) – as it gives a voice in common. Nancy highlights that this is similar to Marx's (1970) idea of a community of literature – a community of articulation rather than organization.

Additionally, Nancy talks of myth and community and advocates that the two are defined by each other. Reflection, through myth, is both the resistance and insistence of community according to Nancy. Myths, he goes on to suggest, mark out the shares and divisions that feature a community and distinguishes itself. Nancy refers to a 'new mythology' through art, aesthetics and creative imagination. Myth, Nancy describes as the will of community and suggests that there is no community outside of myth. In his book, he goes on to state that the interruption of myth, therefore, is also the interruption of community. In this vein, he intimates that community never disappears, but is interrupted through an interruption of myth. It is this notion that Nancy suggests is the basis for Blanchot's unavowable community. Within his discussions of myth, Nancy talks of the fact that myths often are about an isolated hero that makes the community commune. The hero does this usually, Nancy goes on, through communication that he or she effects between existence and meaning and between the individual and the people. Here, then, is one explanation of the ever-present lure of the heroic leader. As Grint (2010b) has pointed out, there is always a draw towards the heroic above ideas of distributed leadership. Nancy appears to give further reason to this assertion.

COMMUNITY AND UNWORKING

For both Blanchot (1988) and Nancy (1991) community cannot exist in the domain of work. Nancy stresses that one does not produce community, one experiences it or is constituted by the experience of its finitude (discussed above). Blanchot proposes community as residing in 'unworking' – that which is before or beyond work. Leadership taken from a community perspective, therefore, based on these notions, would not be part of work, but something akin to a more social domain. Nancy suggests that 'community is given to us with being and as being, well in advance of all our projects, desires, and undertakings' (1991, p. 35) and that community is resistance, the resistance to immanence. Community, Nancy advises, is also what he calls the consumption of a social bond or fabric.

COMMUNITY WITHOUT UNITY

In his book, *Community Without Unity*, Corlett (1989) takes a political view of community and uses Derridian (1978) ideas of extravagance and play (regards Saussure (1966), Pocock (1973), Foucault (1988), Bataille (1970, 1985, 1988) and Connolly (1988) to name but a few references) to problematize the individualistic and collectivist tension in writing and thought around community. He draws on notions of chaos as a part of order to develop a picture of postmodern community and in so doing celebrates both difference and community. In particular, he draws on the Derridian ideas to centralize chaos as a part of order, rather than a marginalized and exiled concept. In this way he critiques ideas of community that exclude and takes difference as a core element of community as a mutual service or strange double-ness. He points out that notions of community express a need to establish unity and uses Michael Taylor's (1982, pp. 26–8) core characteristics of a community (highlighted earlier in the introduction to this book) as an example: (1) persons who compose a community have beliefs and values in common; (2) relations between members should be direct and should be many sided; and (3) reciprocity – mutual aid, cooperation and sharing. Corlett criticizes Taylor's 'exchange' view for draining community of its mystery. In response, he points to community as a mutual appreciation of differences by deconstructing opposites such as meaning/non-meaning, inside/ outside and deconstruction/(re)construction. For instance, he points to distinctions between 'this world' and the 'other world' and that this form of thinking fuels a tension 'between feeling selfish when individualistic and feeling naive when collectivistic' (Corlett, 1989, p. 10).

Here Corlett provides some embodiment of the tension accentuated throughout the community literature of individualistic ideas of leadership and those expressed in more distributed form. As such, he highlights the emotional connective strand between individualism and community in that when 'people become collectivised they hunger for individualism and vice versa' (1989, p. 11). Yet he does not recommend that this is rectified by a pluralistic stance but instead should be taken to celebrate difference as part of community. Here, therefore, for the purpose of this book, the point may be to celebrate difference in leadership construction rather than trying to reconcile difference. As he suggests, he attempts to:

> . . . supplement the politics of sameness and pluralism by locating problems of community within the most extravagant politics of difference possible.

> (Corlett, 1989, p. xix)

In his book Corlett draws out three fundamental themes around a community without unity: subjugation – 'how to live life more fully without abandoning all reason and order' (1989, p. 207); reassurance – which holds up 'the provisional reason and order modernity cannot abandon' (1989, p. 207); giving gifts – 'during which the gift determines identity of the giver and the receiver' (1989, p. 207). This latter point seems central to Corlett's thesis in that he proposes that gift giving is central to the Derridian idea of extravagance, which he draws on to develop notions of community without unity, while also being central to ideas of community itself.

In concluding his book, Corlett describes the work of Berry (1987), where community is seen in historical and economic terms as an insurance, whereby farmers, for instance, could rest assured that other groups nearby could take on work if they were to fall ill. While recognizing this link between groups, Corlett suggests that notions of community now need to develop further and explore other desires people have besides the economic. Corlett points to free gift giving as a way around both Berry's romanticism and Bataille's nihilism (discussed previously through the work of Blanchot and Nancy above). Corlett advises that to live extravagantly is to give gifts freely. He goes on to state:

> Free gift-giving stands beside the reassuring forces of shared oneness and reciprocity in an accidental, silent, extravagant way that strikes with force and interruption until silence is again broken by discourse.
> (Corlett, 1989, p. 202)

He describes this free gift giving as the total immersion of self into community whereby we lose self and he suggests that this mutual service is possible without the unity of having anything in common. Herein, therefore, we might think of leadership as free gift giving, however, the total immersion of leadership into community appears paradoxical. Servant leadership (Greenleaf, 1977) might be mentioned here, yet this concept still marks out the leader in their prominence or character as a heroic figure, elevating the role of servant. This might be where leadership and community part ways as the character of 'leader' cannot be reconciled with community without unity, in the sense that Corlett describes it, as it will always remain conspicuous.

In developing his argument Corlett (1989) also refers to links between politics, community and geography whereby community is used quite often to denote a geographical place. Geography is often taken for granted in ideas of community. This is something that has also been highlighted in the literature on leadership and in particular in research concerned with cross-cultural leadership whereby geographical locations are taken as a proxy for culture, for instance, through the GLOBE project (for example, Chhokar et al., 2007; House et al., 2004), whereas recent calls (for example, Bolden and Kirk, 2009; Edwards, forthcoming; Sveiby, 2011; Turnbull, 2009; Turnbull et al., 2012; Warner and Grint, 2006) hint at a more anthropological and indigenous angle to be developed within the research agenda in leadership and cultural studies.

In addition, in his journey to accentuate a philosophical stance of community without unity, Corlett also underlines briefly the work of Rosenblum (1987), who highlights that community must be seen as beautiful to its members. She uses the work of Walzer (1983) to point to a union that transcends difference of interest drawing on history, culture, religion and language. This also resonates with writing on leadership and takes us back to the need for an aesthetic appreciation of leadership that is derived from cultural and historical foundations that are deeply rooted in language and religion.

ETHICAL COMMUNITY

In the latter chapters of his book, Bauman (2001) calls for the widening of a scope for ethical community and discusses philosophical notions of human rights in this regard. He shows that this form of community is based on foundations of fraternity and common interest. He suggests that the modern day slotting people into ethnic minorities against their will masks these ideas of common interest, fraternity and hence an ethical community. Instead he stresses the importance of place and space and a sense of belonging, already discussed in Chapters 5 and 2, respectively. Bauman uses the work of Richard Sennett (1999) to describe how an experience of belonging is linked to geographical places such as nations, towns and cities. Bauman goes on to describe a sense of place being linked to a need to belong to 'society', yet society is an imagined entity. He signals that society is linked to images of a 'caring and sharing community' that resonates security. Bauman concludes his book by suggesting that:

We miss community because we miss security, a quality crucial to a happy life, but one which the world we inhabit is ever less able to offer and ever more reluctant to promise. But community remains stubbornly missing . . .

(Bauman, 2001, p. 144)

He suggests, as a final comment, that if community is to exist in a world of individuals then it can only be 'a community woven together from sharing and mutual care . . .' (2001, p. 150). As a last comment for this chapter, it seems resonant to draw parallels with the emerging literature on leadership as having a duty of care (Cuilla, 2009; Gabriel, forthcoming).

SUMMARY

This chapter has reviewed postmodern perspectives of community and related them to the leadership literature. By conducting this review the chapter has highlighted the importance of taking a discursive viewpoint when researching leadership. The chapter has stressed issues of friendship, fluidity, finitude, love and death that also have relative importance to studying leadership. The chapter ends with a core theme throughout this book – ethics – and reiterates those calling for leadership to have a duty and an ethic of care.

Concluding remarks

Writing this book has been a long journey and I have found immense enjoyment in immersing myself in a new body of literature and attempting to connect this with leadership studies. I hope you have found the book useful in your own journey within the world of leadership research. This chapter is meant as a place to end the journey of writing and a place to reflect on the contribution of the book and future avenues for research, methodology and leadership learning and development. There are many reflections made within the book and I will not attempt to capture all, but reflect on some key observations and connections I have made while re-reading various chapters.

KEY POINTS OF REFERENCE FOR LEADERSHIP RESEARCH

First, the book seems to point quite strongly towards a relational and socially constructed view of leadership. This appears to be both relational in the sense of leader-follower relations, but also relational in the sense of leader-follower and the community. Seeing self in community has been highlighted as an important angle for leadership study (for example, Bolden and Kirk, 2009; Edwards, forthcoming), and this book has argued in favour of an extension of the concept of leader-follower in relation to community.

It also appears that deeper appreciation of connections of individualism to leadership, and the complexity of notions of individualism need to be developed. The recommendation of this book is to do this through the paradigm of character, caricature and costume. In a sense, therefore, this draws on notions of fluidity and especially the fluidity of leadership identity and, in particular, linked to space and place. Doing so will develop more in-depth contextual interpretations of leadership. Harnessing the fluid ideas of modernity (for example, Bauman, 2000, 2001; Maffesoli, 1996), therefore, seems to be a key challenge for the future of leadership research.

The book has also uncovered a better appreciation of a sense of belonging linked to leadership, uncovering an inherent multiple belonging (for example, Maffesoli, 1996) perspective that provides contextual richness to the study of leadership, taking into account fluidity, the senses and cultural complexity. Exploring more socio-logical interpretations of belonging (for example, May, 2011) linked to notions of leadership appears to be an important line of further reflection and research.

In addition, the book seems to underline the importance of taking an aesthetic outlook when considering the social construction of leadership. Taking leadership as a symbolic representation of group activity appears to be important and could lead to interesting avenues for research into ideas such as aesthetic frill and leadership as ritual.

The book seems also to drift naturally towards an ethical explora-tion of leadership. This viewpoint appears connected intrinsically to ideas of community, but should also be seen in a fluid and critical lens, where ethics are derived from the community through language and discourse as opposed to being tenants of living a life as a leader. The duty of care notion of leadership too seems to resonate well with leadership built from a community view.

REFLECTIONS ON LEADERSHIP LEARNING AND DEVELOPMENT

In certain places in the book reference is made to my own experience of designing and facilitating leadership development and learning interventions. It therefore seems important to try and summarize some key points here. One key aspect that the book stresses is the idea of friendship within leadership learning. In Chapter 3 the topics of friendship and betrayal were highlighted as key components of self. If leadership development is to see a clear link with self-development, then a deeper appreciation of more socially orientated concepts such as friendship and betrayal needs to be incorporated into the design and delivery of such programmes. Leadership development, therefore, could be argued to focus more on friend-ship development (with an appreciation of betrayal) rather than self-development, as self-development is dependent on friendship. How many times as leadership developers have we seen or heard that delegates and students have become life-long friends owing to experiences on such programmes? I, myself, have heard this many times and yet there is a lack of appreciation as to the conceptual importance of friendship in the mechanism of leadership learning and development. Also recognizing betrayal as inherent in a leader-ship relationship, similar to observations by Krantz (2006), seems to be important for the future of leadership learning. For example, how can leadership development programmes enable leaders to cope with betrayal? What mechanisms can be developed to recognize and react to acts of betraying and being betrayed?

Second, it appears from discussions in this book that leadership learning and development should emphasize a more embodied and material sense. As Sinclair (2005) has highlighted, recognizing the body in leadership learning through more acute observation of gesture, stature and voice, for example, seems paramount. Added to this is the observation that better recognition of the impact of place and space within the learning process and how this relates to observations of embodied leadership will also enhance learning for leaders.

Last, leadership learning and development might look towards enabling those assigned with leadership roles to reflect on the characters and caricatures they portray. Related to the embodied discussion above is the role of costume and a wider appreciation that appearance generally will better serve would-be leader than searching for a one true self. Instead drawing on differing notions of individualism and how this connects to community and leadership might help develop contextually rich notions of leadership in the learning environment.

LEADERSHIP AND CONTEXT

At the very start of this book I indicated that by looking at leadership through the lens of community one might gain a better understand-ing of leadership in context. What seems to have emerged from the review and reflection are areas where notions of leadership are likely to be constructed in response to context and environmental factors. This ultimately helps the researcher in the search for leadership to target certain contextual spaces. For example, a lot of what is dis-cussed in this book relates leadership to large-scale social constructs that are inherently tension ridden. It appears that leadership is most likely constructed in cracks, gaps and edges within and between these concepts. To further exemplify this point it is interesting to note that in one or two places in this book leadership is related to boundaries within and between communities and therefore it seems that leadership is most likely constructed at the point of boundary and, as I allude to in Chapter 5, as an aesthetic frill to the group and a symbolic representation of the boundary. This directs us to explore the contextualization of leadership at the edges. Here it could be useful to draw on Kanter's (1972) ideas of permeability, the degree to which community boundaries are open and permit penetration of movement across them. Permeability also enables communities to gather information and feedback and aids dealings with the environment through the creation of boundary roles. This then presents an example of how and where leadership might be constructed on the edge of a community and the concept of permeability as the driving force behind such a construction. Here, therefore, we see leadership as community or group permeability.

SO WHAT FOR STUDYING LEADERSHIP?

As already stated, this book takes a community perspective on leadership and thus provides some theoretical suggestions regarding the conceptualization of leadership that in turn may inform future research approaches to leadership. This book also represents a methodology for studying leadership. Similar to the concept of 'The Leaderful Moment' (Wood and Ladkin, 2008), the foray into ideas of community can provide the foundation for a discussion on how to approach the actual study of leadership. This is evident in the literature on leadership and the concept of the 'Leaderful Moment', for instance, is the epitome of this argument. The concept of the 'Leaderful Moment' indicates using 'frames of leadership' (using photography, film, art) to develop an understanding of leadership in the moment. This is ultimately a methodology for investigating leadership in context and provides a broader view of what leadership is or could be based on geography (place and space), history, context and culture. Similarly, previous reflections on community and distributed leadership have suggested ways to study leadership as listed in Table 1. This perspective also seems linked to ideas represented by

Table 1   *Concepts of community, distributed leadership and research implications*

Concept of community	Link to distributed leadership	Research implications
Symbolism	Relates through the aesthetic; sees distributed leadership as represented by the symbolic construction of boundaries	Calls for an aesthetic form of methodology. For example, using the 'Leaderful Moment' method highlighted by Wood and Ladkin (2008)
Sense of belonging	Suggests a co-constructed mutual sense of belonging based on cultural connections	Could be investigated through methodologies that develop an understanding of a connective sense of belonging. Calls for a methodology that develops a group-based inquiry over time; could also involve observation-based data
Sense of community	Would be based on a mutual sense of a supportive network of relationships (relates to a sense of belonging)	Could use frameworks such as membership, influence, integration and fulfilment of needs and shared emotional connection (McMillan and Chavis, 1986). Because related to a sense of belonging, could usefully explore parallels and differences between the two
Individualism	Brings out the tension between a shared sense of identity and individual self-identity	Could use co-produced auto-ethnographic forms of research (similar to Kempster and Stewart's (2010) research on leadership development). Could explore how these tensions materialize in the construction of self in relation to context

Concept of community	Link to distributed leadership	Research implications
Community as communicative	Involves understanding distributed leadership from the perspective of common values, ethics and morals	Co-produced auto-ethnographic forms of research would highlight tensions between individually held beliefs and how these inter-relate with contextual group norms (there is an overlap here with ethical leadership research)
Language	Notion of distributed leadership as bounded by language, discourse and dialect	Understanding how leadership is conceptualized within and through differing languages and for different contexts to uncover latent constructs. Qualitative investigation based on word usage, meaning and enactment
Liminality	Suggests that notions of distributed leadership may be virtual, contextually bound, fluid and shifting based on ideas of space and place	Ethnographic to enable an understanding of leadership situated in context and time. Could be centred on specific tasks or projects in organizations to gain a sense of the shifting, rotating basis of leadership. Artistic or aesthetic forms of data collection could help to represent the fluidity of distributed leadership by giving research participants a broader scope to explore interpretations of leadership

Table 1 continued

Concept of community	Link to distributed leadership	Research implications
Friendship	Suggests an informal notion of distributed leadership linked to social networks	An ethnographic approach might make it possible to uncover social networks within organizations and the impact on how decisions are made or not made. Demands an ability to 'go behind the scenes' of the formal organizational structure to uncover underlying social and friendship networks. Need to collect data within and outside the organization in more social settings (for example, Sturdy et al., 2006)
The postmodern community	Highlights distributed leadership as inter-connected multi-distributed; individuals are members of a number of differing forms of distributed leadership based on emotional connections	Implications from all other concepts could be relevant here, as the issues of community, in the context of postmodernity, apply throughout

Source: Edwards (2011, p. 308).

Turner (1967) of exhibition and maybe researching leadership as an exhibition rather than an individual might enable broad as well as rich interpretations.

It would appear that from my original publication in 2011, further additional recommendations for methods of studying leadership appear merited based on the discussion in this book. For instance, taking inspiration from Greg Urban (1996), leadership researchers might develop stronger analysis based on discourse, sensory, myth and narrative analysis. It seems these forms of data collection and analysis would help re-embody ideas of leadership and move us away from representation of individualized leaders and leadership.

Also, the ethnographic investigation of leadership might also benefit from seeing leadership as a social drama, and see space and place as a key aspect of the contextualization of leadership. Last, seeking out what it is we, as a community, society or organization, want from leadership as opposed to a prescribed framework of leadership might help us drive leadership as community within our research agendas.

WHAT HASN'T THIS BOOK COVERED?

Although I do draw on the writing and research of some female scholars (for example, De Wolfe, 2002; Kamau, 2002; Kanter, 1972; Love Brown, 2002; Rosenblum, 1987), the book tends to draw primarily on male voices. Philosophers and community writers and academics I have related to in the process of developing themes for this book are mostly, if not mainly, male. I am thus concerned as to whether the female voice is undermined in this work and would signal this as a critical area for further reflection and debate.

I am also aware that in places the book does tend towards the overly positive with regards to community in the sense of seeing community as ultimately desirable. While I have attempted to represent counter arguments and discussion where possible, I feel this is an area for further critical discussion, reflection and debate. Additionally, there are concepts that appear linked to community that would benefit from further reflection regarding their links to leadership. Aspects such as trust and wisdom (highlighted in the friendship literature – Phal, 2000), social bond (Urban, 1996), alliance theory (Urban, 1996), cultural studies (for example, Fiske and Hartley, 1978; Hall and Jefferson, 1976; Hebdige, 1979), sources of self (for example, Taylor, 1989), *jouissance* (Blanchot, 1988; Nancy, 1991), compearance (Nancy, 1991), commitment (Kanter, 1972), difference (Derrida, 1978), isomorphism (Kanter, 1972), Sociogenesis (the development of mutual relationships in groups) (for example, Andelson, 2002) and Schismogenesis (the breach between sub-groups) (for example, Andelson, 2002; Bateson, 1936, 1972, 1979) are areas I have identified as part of my research into the subject of community and leadership. Further explorations of these notions linked to leadership appear, on the surface at least, to be useful contributions to the ongoing research.

Kinship is a further idea that has been underlined in some of the texts to which I have found myself drawn (for example, Urban, 1996). This area could also be developed further in connection to leadership, as could the use of narrative analysis (Urban, 1996). Also linked to the idea of leadership and community as discourse, there appears to be connection to the idea of mimetics and I would therefore argue in favour of further reflection around mimetics and leadership as a meme (see Blackmore, 1999; Dawkins, 1989). Last, I am not sure that I have fully explored the contributions of some of the postmodern and modernist writings on community such as Blanchot (1988), Nancy (1991), Lash (1994) and Agamben (1993). With regards to Agamben, there are some concepts that I believe could develop the thinking about leadership further, such as 'being-such', 'linguistic-being', 'being-called' and 'being-in-act'. While I reflect on some of these concepts in the book, further reflection on these works will, I am sure, take up my time in the future and hopefully others will be inspired to do so as well.

In addition, Chapter 6 has concentrated on MacIntyre's notions of 'character', 'role' and 'tradition' in connecting with the leadership and community literature. At this point it is important to note other concepts he explores such as practice, episodes, narrative and quests. Future consideration in this area should develop these concepts in connection with community perspectives of leadership. Also, other writers seem to have a connection to this theme of community, ethics and leadership, not least the writing of John MacMurry (see Weir, 2012). Indeed, Ricoeur (1992) discusses 'character' in his work, which is empirically developed by Cunliffe and Eriksen (2011) whereby they recognize the character not as traits or constructs but as being embedded and expressed within conversation. A possible future orientation would be to compare notions of character developed in the study conducted by Cunliffe and Eriksen with the ideas of Ricoeur and MacIntyre.

In addition, there has been some research into the meaning of ethics in differing countries (for example, Resick et al., 2011). However, further development of this work along an emic or worldliness outlook (Mintzberg and Gosling, 2003; Turnbull, 2009; Turnbull et al., 2012) would add to this area of community and leadership research in relation to ethics from an inter-cultural frame.

It appears that if one is to make suggestions around the future of leadership studies then it seems there needs to be a reconciliation of current contemporary ideals of business leadership with a community-based philosophy. This, it appears, needs to be contextually bound in the sense of developing an understanding of how leadership and ethics are framed by the 'character', 'role' and 'tradition' of leadership. As Maffesoli (1996) points out through Renan (1984), the ancient god is neither good nor bad but a force. Maffesoli goes on to recommend that this is not a moralizing force but a force expressed through differing characters and suggests a pluralistic view of ethics that cannot be resolved through the constraints of one-dimensional science. Bringing leadership closer to community perspectives through an appreciation of symbolism, language, friendship, belonging and liminality in constructing ideals of ethics and leadership therefore appears important. This might be done practically through enacting a 'Secret Millionaire' and back-to-the-floor type exercises, such as 'Undercover Boss' (both are popular television programmes in the US and UK) within leadership development programmes. This is where positional leadership are given community projects to work on and fund or where they visit the lower levels and branches of the organization to experience the contexts and environments in differing parts of society and their own organization. It is this type of reconciliation of individualistic identity derived from business success and the reconnection with society that may be a viable option in developing leadership and ethics in contemporary organizations.

WHERE NEXT FOR A COMMUNITY-BASED PERSPECTIVE ON LEADERSHIP?

This book represents an initial development of themes linked to leadership from the community literature. The community literature, like the leadership literature, however, appears to have a distinct American flavour, sometimes explicitly so. For instance, the work by Paul Lichterman (1996) discusses political community from a very forthright American frame. Other influences for the book such as Joseph Guisfield and Alasdair MacIntyre are scholars discussing concepts from either an explicitly or implicitly American paradigm. The ideas represented in this book therefore could be developed further by understanding other community perspectives that are derived from a less American viewpoint. Indeed, as has been critiqued at the beginning of the book, the leadership literature is far too Westernized and Americanized. While attempting to redress the balance with this book, there is the argument that the community literature used is still derived from Western and American ideals. Also, it would appear that the very notion of community could be a Western or an American construct. Or, alternatively, the community literature may be represented as some postcolonial rationalization of society, which hopes to draw on wisdom from the wider world, yet resides still in the American ideal. Either way I feel troubled by this and argue that we need to have further research that investigates and understands differing notions of the community ideal from around the world. Here we might take interesting work from the leadership literature that is of a more anthropological frame (for example, Edwards, forthcoming; Harter, 2006; Jones, 2005, Sveiby, 2011) and reframe the focus to understand community alongside leadership as opposed to the focus taken by this book, which is to understand leadership through community.

Last, the link between leader, character and caricature merits further reflection and it seems that there are at least three areas that could be developed. The first is to further explore 'character'. To do so writers such as Richard Sennett, and his work about the corrosion of character (1998), and C. Wright Mills, and his work on character and social structure (with Hans Gerth) (Gerth and Wright Mills, 1954) seem important. These two pieces of work appear to stress an appreciation of character as a construct in the social sciences and hence may provide further illumination regarding the idea of character and linking to leadership, especially ethical leadership. Second, themes from the performing arts and creative arts literature about character and caricature development to develop notions around how ethical leadership and leadership more generally are processed into character and caricature formats. What's more, such research should reflect on issues of organizational practice and in particular repercussion for leadership development and learning. Last, further research is needed to incorporate a wider discussion on the use of metaphors and further appreciation of Alvesson and Spicer's work on metaphors of leadership. In particular a link can be made with the preceding discussion regarding character and caricature development and how Alvesson and Spicer are creating characters and caricatures for the management world.

References

Acevedo, B. (2011). 'The screaming Pope: imagery and leadership in two paintings of the Pope Innocent X'. *Leadership*, 7, 27–50.

Agamben, G. (1993). *The Coming Community*. Minneapolis, MN: University of Minnesota Press.

Ahonen, P., D. Knights and P. Case (2012). 'Leadership. Ethics and the modalities of power'. Paper presented at the 28th European Group for Organisation Studies (EGOS) Colloquium, Helsinki, Finland, 5–7 July.

Alvesson, M. and A. Spicer (2010). *Metaphors We Lead By*. London: Routledge.

Alvesson, M. and S. Sveningsson (2003). 'Managers doing leadership: the extra-ordinarization of the mundane'. *Human Relations*, **56**(12), 1435–59.

Andelson, J.G. (2002). 'Coming together and breaking apart: sociogenesis and schismogenesis in intentional communities'. In S. Love Brown (ed.), *Intentional Community: An Anthropological Perspective*. New York: State University of New York Press, pp. 131–52.

Anderman, L.H. (1999). 'Classroom goal orientation, school belonging and social goals as predictors of students' positive and negative affect following the transition to middle school'. *Journal of Research and Development in Education*, **32**, 89–103.

Anderson, B. (1983). *Imagined Communities*. London: Verso, reprinted in 2006.

Avolio, B.J. and W.L. Gardner (2005). 'Authentic leadership development: getting to the root of positive forms of leadership'. *Leadership Quarterly*, **16**(3), 315–38.

Avolio, B.J., W.L. Gardner, F.O. Walumbwa, F. Luthans and D.R. May (2004). 'Unlocking the mask: a look at the process by which authentic leaders impact follower attitudes and behaviours'. *Leadership Quarterly*, **15**, 801–23.

Bales, N. (1989). *A Sense of Belonging.* Nashville, TN: 20th Century Christian Foundation.

Balkundi, P. and M. Kilduff (2006). 'The ties that bind: a social network approach to leadership'. *Leadership Quarterly*, **17**, 419–39.

Barker, P. (2012). *Hebden Bridge: A Sense of Belonging.* London: Francis Lincoln.

Barry, D. and S. Meisiek (2010). 'The art of leadership and its fine art shadow'. *Leadership*, **6**(2), 331–49.

Bass, B.M. (1985). *Leadership and Performance Beyond Expectations.* New York: The Free Press.

Bass, B.M. and R. Riggio (2006). *Transformational Leadership*, second edn. Mahwah, NJ: Lawrence Erlbaum Associates.

Bass, B.M. and P. Steidlmeier (1999). 'Ethics, character and authentic transformational leadership behaviour'. *Leadership Quarterly*, **10**, 181–21.

Bass, B.M. and R. Stogdill (1990). *Bass and Stogdill's Handbook of Leadership: Theory, Research and Managerial Applications.* New York: The Free Press.

Bass, B.M., D.A. Waldman, B.J. Avolio and M. Bebb (1987). 'Transformational leadership and the falling dominoes effect'. *Group and Organization Studies*, **12**, 73–87.

Bastien, A. (1881). *Der Völkergedanke im Aufbau einer Wissenschaft vom Menschen: und seine Begründung auf ethnologische Sammlungen.* Berlin: Dümmlers.

Bataille, G. (1970). *Oeuvres Complétes.* Vol. 1. Paris: Gallimard.

Bataille, G. (1985). *Visions of Excess: Selected Writings, 1927–39*, trans. A. Stoekl. Minneapolis, MN: University of Minnesota Press.

Bataille, G. (1988). *Inner Experience*, trans. L. Boldt. Albany, NY: State University of New York Press.

Bateson, G. (1936). *Naven.* Palo Alto, CA: Stanford University Press.

Bateson, G. (1972). *Steps to an Ecology of the Mind.* Chicago, IL: University of Chicago Press.

Bateson, G. (1979). *Mind and Nature.* New York: E.P. Dutton.

Bathurst, R. and N. Monin (2010). 'Shaping leadership for today: Mary Parker Follett's aesthetic'. *Leadership*, **6**(2), 115–31.

Bathurst, R., B. Jackson and M. Statler (2010). 'Leading aesthetically in uncertain times'. *Leadership*, **6**, 311–30.

Bauman, Z. (2000). *Liquid Modernity.* Cambridge: Polity Press.

Bauman, Z. (2001). *Community: Seeking Safety in an Unsecure World.* Cambridge: Polity Press.

Beech, N. (2011). 'Liminality and the practices of identity construction'. *Human Relations*, **64**(2), 285–302.

Bell, D. (1976). *The Cultural Contradictions of Capitalism.* New York: Basic Books.

Bellah, R. (1985). *Habits of the Heart.* Oakland, CA: University of California Press.

Benne, K.D. and P. Sheats (1948). 'Functional roles of group members'. *Journal of Social Issues*, **4**(2), 41–9.

Bennis, W.G. (1984). 'The 4 competencies of leadership'. *Training & Development Journal*, August, 17.

Bennis, W.G. (1989). *On Becoming a Leader.* Philadelphia, PA: Perseus Books.

Bennis, W.G. and B. Nanus (1985). *Leaders: The Strategies for Taking Charge.* New York: Harper & Row.

Bennis, W.G. and R.J. Thomas (2002). *Geeks and Geezers.* Boston, MA: Harvard Business School Press.

Berry, W. (1987). *Home Economics.* San Francisco, CA: North Point Press.

Blackmore, S. (1999). *The Meme Machine.* Oxford: Oxford University Press.

Blanchot, M. (1988). *The Unavowable Community.* Barrytown, NY: Station Hill Press.

Blum, L.A. (1980). *Friendship, Altruism and Morality.* London: Routledge.

Bolden, R. (2011). 'Distributed leadership in organisations: a review of theory and research'. *International Journal of Management Reviews*, **13**(3), 251–69.

Bolden, R. and J. Gosling (2006). 'Leadership competencies: time to change the tune?', *Leadership*, **2**(2), 147–63.

Bolden, R. and P. Kirk (2009). 'African leadership: surfacing new understandings through leadership development'. *International Journal of Cross Cultural Management*, **9**, 69–86.

Bolden, R., G. Petrov and J. Gosling (2008). *Developing Collective Leadership in Higher Education.* London: Leadership Foundation for Higher Education.

Bradbury, H. and B.M. Lichtenstein (2000). 'Relationality in organisational research: exploring the space between'. *Organisation Science*, **11**, 551–64.

Brass, D.J., J. Galakiewicz, H.R. Greve and W. Tsai (2004). 'Taking stock of networks and organizations: a multilevel perspective'. *Academy of Management Journal*, **47**, 795–817.

Broadie, S. and C. Rowe (2002). *Aristotle, Nicomachean Ethics: Translation, Introduction and Commentary*. Oxford: Oxford University Press.

Brown, M.E. and L.K. Treviño (2006). 'Ethical leadership: a review and future directions'. *Leadership Quarterly*, **17**, 595–616.

Brown, M.E., L.K. Treviño and D.A. Harrison (2005). 'Ethical leadership: a social learning perspective for construct development and testing'. *Organisational Behaviour and Human Decision Processes*, **97**, 117–34.

Bruhn, J.G. (2008). 'The functionality of gray area ethics in organisations'. *Journal of Business Ethics*, **89**(2), 204–14.

Burns, J.M. (1978). *Leadership*. New York: Harper & Row.

Burns, J.M. (2005). 'Leadership'. *Leadership*, **1**(1), 11–12.

Carnegie, D. (1936). *How to Win Friends and Influence People*. New York: Simon and Schuster.

Caza, A. and B. Jackson (2011). 'Authentic leadership'. In A. Bryman, D. Collinson, K. Grint, B. Jackson and M. Uhl-Bien (eds), *The Sage Handbook of Leadership*. London: Sage, pp. 353–64.

Chapple, E.D. and C.S. Coon (1942). *Principles of Anthropology*. New York: Henry Holt and Company.

Chemers, M.M., C.B. Watson and S.T. May (2000). 'Dispositional affect and leadership effectiveness: a comparison of self-esteem, optimism and efficacy'. *Personality and Social Psychology Bulletin*, **26**(3), 267–77.

Chhokar, J.S., F.C. Brodbeck and R.J. House (eds) (2007). *Culture and Leadership Across the World: The GLOBE Book of In Depth Studies of 25 Societies*. Mahwah, NJ: Lawrence Erlbaum.

Ciulla, J.B. (ed.) (2004a). *Ethics: The Heart of Leadership*, second edn. Westport, CT: Praeger.

Ciulla, J.B. (2004b). 'Ethics and leadership effectiveness'. In J. Antonakis, A.T. Cianciolo and R.J. Sternberg (eds), *The Nature of Leadership*. Thousand Oaks, CA: Sage, pp. 302–27.

Ciulla, J.B. (2009). 'Leadership and the ethics of care'. *Journal of Business Ethics*, **88**(1), 3–4.

Ciulla, J.B. (2012). 'Ethics and effectiveness: the nature of good leadership'. In D.V. Day and J. Antonakis (eds), *The Nature of Leadership*, second edn. Los Angeles, CA: Sage, pp. 508–40.

Ciulla, J.B. (2013). 'Searching for Mandela: the saint as a sinner who keeps on trying'. In D. Ladkin and C. Spiller (eds), *Authentic Leadership: Clashes, Convergences and Coalescences.* Northampton, MA, USA and Cheltenham, UK: Edward Elgar, pp. 152–75.

Ciulla, J.B. and D.R. Forsyth (2011). 'Leadership ethics'. In A. Bryman, D. Collinson, K. Grint, B. Jackson and M. Uhl-Bien (eds), *The Sage Handbook of Leadership.* London: Sage, pp. 229–41.

Clark, P. and M. Rowlinson (2004). 'The treatment of history in organisation studies: towards an "historic turn"?'. *Business History*, **46**(3), 331–52.

Clarke, C., C. Kelliher and D. Schedlitzki (2013). 'Labouring under false pretences? The emotional labour of authentic leadership'. In D. Ladkin and C. Spiller (eds), *Authentic Leadership: Clashes, Convergences and Coalescences.* Northampton, MA, USA and Cheltenham, UK: Edward Elgar, pp. 75–92.

Cobban, A. (1964). *The Social Interpretation of the French Revolution.* Cambridge: Cambridge University Press.

Cohen, A.P. (1985). *The Symbolic Construction of Community.* New York: Routledge.

Collinge, C. and J. Gibney (2011). 'Connecting place, policy and leadership'. In C. Collinge, J. Gibney and C. Mabey (eds), *Leadership and Place.* New York: Routledge, pp. 13–26.

Collinge, C., J. Gibney and C. Mabey (eds) (2011). *Leadership and Place.* New York: Routledge.

Collinson, D. (2005). 'Dialectics of leadership'. *Human Relations*, **58**(11), 1419–22.

Collinson, D. (2012). 'Prozac leadership and the limits of positive thinking'. *Leadership*, **8**(2), 87–107.

Conger, J.A. and R.N. Kanungo (1987). 'Toward a behavioural theory of charismatic leadership in organisational settings'. *Academy of Management Review*, **13**, 471–82.

Conger, J.A. and R.A. Kanungo (1998). *Charismatic Leadership in Organisations.* Thousand Oaks, CA: Sage.

Connell, J. and J. Wellborn (1991). 'Competence, autonomy and relatedness: a motivational analysis of self-system processes'. In M.R. Gunnar and L.A. Sroufe (eds), *Self-processes and Development.* Hillsdale, NJ: Erlbaum, pp. 43–77.

Conner, P. (1991). 'Preface'. In J.-L. Nancy (ed.), *The Inoperative Community.* Minneapolis, MN: University of Minnesota Press, pp. xxxvi–xli.

Connolly, W. (1988). *Political Theory and Modernity.* Oxford: Basil Blackwell.

Corlett, W. (1989). *Community Without Unity: A Politics of Derridan Extravagance.* Durham, NC: Duke University Press.

Cresswell, T. (2004). *Place: A Short Introduction.* Oxford: Blackwell.

Cunha, M.P., N. Guimarães-Costa, A. Rego and S.R. Clegg (2010). 'Leading and following (un)ethically in *Limen*'. *Journal of Business Ethics*, **97**, 189–206.

Cunliffe, A.L. and M. Eriksen (2011). 'Relational leadership'. *Human Relations*, **64**(11), 1425–49.

Currie, G., A. Lockett and O. Suhomlinova (2009). 'The institutionalization of distributed leadership: a "Catch-22" in English public services'. *Human Relations*, **62**, 1735–61.

Curtis, R. (2013). 'A study of implicit leadership theories among business and management undergraduate students'. Unpublished Masters of Research (MRes) Thesis, University of Gloucestershire, Cheltenham, UK.

Czarniawska, B. and C. Mazza (2003). 'Consulting as liminal space'. *Human Relations*, **56**(3), 267–90.

Dawkins, R. (1989). *The Selfish Gene.* Oxford: Oxford University Press.

De Cremer, D. and H.J.E.M. Alberts (2004). 'When procedural fairness does not influence how positive I feel: the effects of voice and leader selection as a function of belongingness need'. *European Journal of Social Psychology*, **34**, 333–44.

De Cremer, D., B. van Kippenberg, D. van Kippenberg, D. Mullenders and F. Stinglhamber (2005). 'Rewarding leadership and fair procedures as determinants of self esteem'. *Journal of Applied Psychology*, **90**(1), 3–12.

De Wolfe, E. (2002). 'The mob at Enfield: community, gender, and violence against the Shakers'. In S. Love Brown (ed.), *Intentional Community: An Anthropological Perspective.* New York: State University of New York Press, pp. 107–30.

Delanty, G. (2003). *Community.* Abingdon: Routledge, reprinted in 2010.

DeLillo, D. (1971). *Americana.* London: Penguin.

Den Hartog, D.N. and M.W. Dickson (2004). 'Leadership and culture'. In J. Antonakis, A.T. Cianciolo and R.J. Sternberg (eds), *The Nature of Leadership.* Thousand Oaks, CA: Sage, pp. 249–78.

Denning, S. (2004). *Squirrel Inc. A Fable of Leadership through Storytelling.* San Francisco, CA: Jossey-Bass.

Denning, S. (2005). *The Leader's Guide to Storytelling: Mastering the Art and Discipline of Business Narrative.* San Francisco, CA: Jossey-Bass.

Derrida, J. (1978). *Writing and Difference*, translated by A. Bass. Chicago, IL: University of Chicago Press.

Derrida, J. (1988). 'The politics of friendship'. *Journal of Philosophy*, **85**(11), 632–44.

Derrida, J. (1997). *The Politics of Friendship.* London: Verso.

Donaldson, T. and T.W. Dunfee (1994). 'Toward a unified conception of business ethics: integrative social contracts theory'. *Academy of Management Review*, **19**(2), 252–84.

Downing, F. (2003). 'Transcending memory: remembrance and the design of place'. *Design Studies*, **24**, 213–35.

Downton, J.V. (1973). *Rebel Leadership.* New York: The Free Press.

Durkheim, E. (1897). *Suicide: A Study in Sociology.* New York: The Free Press, reprinted in 1951.

Durkheim, E. (1964). *The Division of Labour in Society.* New York: The Free Press.

Edwards, D. (1995). 'The school counselor's role in helping teachers and students'. *Elementary School Guidance and Counseling*, **29**, 191–7.

Edwards, G.P. (2011). 'Concepts of community: a framework for contextualising distributed leadership'. *International Journal of Management Reviews*, **13**(3), 301–12.

Edwards, G.P. (2012). 'Worldly leadership and concepts of community'. In S. Turnbull, P. Case, G. Edwards, D. Jepson and P. Simpson (eds), *Worldly Leadership.* London: Palgrave Macmillan, pp. 85–101.

Edwards, G.P. (forthcoming). 'Anthropological accounts of leadership: historical and geographical interpretations from indigenous cultures'. *Leadership.* Expected publication August 2015, available on onlinefirst at http://lea.sagepub.com/content/early/recent until that date.

Edwards, G.P., P.K. Winter and J. Bailey (2002). *Leadership in Management.* Ross-on-Wye: The Leadership Trust Foundation.

Edwards, G.P., D. Schedlitzki, J. Ward and M. Wood (forthcoming a). 'Exploring critical perspectives of toxic and bad leadership through film'. *Advances in Developing Human Resources*,

Special Issue on Creative Techniques in Leadership Learning and Development.

Edwards, G.P., D. Schedlitzki, S. Turnbull and R. Gill (forthcoming b). 'Exploring power assumptions in the leadership and management debate'. *Leadership and Organisation Development Journal.*

Emanuelli, H. (2010). *A Sense of Belonging: From the Rhondda to the Potteries.* Langenfeld, Germany: Six Towns Books.

Etzioni, A. (1993). *The Spirit of Community.* London: Harper Collins.

Faircloth, B.S. and J.V. Hamm (2005). 'Sense of belonging among high school students representing four ethnic groups'. *Journal of Youth and Adolescence*, **34**(4), 293–309.

Fairhurst, G. (2007). *Discursive Leadership: In Conversation with Leadership Psychology.* Thousand Oaks, CA: Sage.

Fiske, A. (1961). 'Saint Anselm'. *Studia Monastica*, **3**(2), 259–90.

Fiske, J. and J. Hartley (1978). *Reading Television.* London: Methuen.

Ford, J. (2010). 'Studying leadership critically: a psychosocial lens on leadership identities'. *Leadership*, **6**(1), 47–65.

Ford. J. and N. Harding (2007). 'Move over management; we are all leaders now'. *Management Learning*, **38**(5), 475–93.

Ford, J., N. Harding and M. Learmonth (2008). *Leadership as Identity.* Basingstoke: Palgrave Macmillan.

Fortier, A.M. (2000). *Migrant Belongings: Memory, Space, Identity.* Oxford: Berg.

Foster, L. (2002). 'Between two worlds: community, liminality, and the development of alternative marriage systems'. In S. Love Brown (ed.), *Intentional Community: An Anthropological Perspective.* New York: State University of New York Press, pp. 67–82.

Foucault, M. (1988). 'The ethics of care for the self as a practice of freedom', trans. J.D. Gauthier. In J. Bernauer and D. Rasmussen (eds), *The Final Foucault.* Cambridge, MA: MIT Press, pp.1–20.

Fraisse, J.-C. (1974). *Philia: La Notion d'Amitie dans la Philosophie Antique.* Paris: Librairie Philosophique J. Vrin.

Freeman, T.M., L.H. Anderman and J.M. Jensen (2007). 'Sense of belonging in college freshmen at the classroom and campus levels'. *Journal of Experimental Education*, **75**(3), 203–20.

French, R. (2007). 'Friendship and organization: learning from the Western friendship tradition'. *Management and Organizational History*, **2**, 255–72.

French, R. (2008). 'Sharing thoughts on leadership and friendship'. In J.K. Turnbull and J. Collins (eds), *Leadership Perspectives: Knowledge into Action.* Basingstoke: Palgrave Macmillan, pp. 43–57.

French, R., P. Case and J. Gosling (2009). 'Betrayal and friendship'. *Society and Business Review*, **4**, 146–58.

Friedrich, T.L., W.B. Vessey, M.J. Schuelke, M.D. Mumford, F.J. Yammarino and G.A. Ruark (2014). 'Collectivist leadership and George C. Marshall: a historiometric analysis of career events.' *Leadership Quarterly*, **25**, 449–67.

Fynsk, C. (1991). 'Foreword'. In J.-L. Nancy (ed.), *The Inoperative Community.* Minneapolis, MN: University of Minnesota Press, pp vii–xxxv.

Gabriel, Y. (forthcoming). 'The caring leader: what followers expect of their leader and why'. *Leadership.* Expected publication August 2015, available on onlinefirst at http://lea.sagepub.com/content/early/recent until that date.

Gans, H.J. (1988). *Middle American Individualism: The Future of Liberal Democracy.* New York: The Free Press.

Gardner, W.L., B.J. Avolio, F. Luthans, D.R. May and F. Walumbwa (2005). 'Can you see the real me? A self based model of authentic leader and follower development'. *Leadership Quarterly*, **16**(3), 343–72.

Gardner, W.L., C.C. Cogliser, K.M. Davis and M.P. Dickens (2011). 'Authentic leadership: a review of the literature and research agenda'. *Leadership Quarterly*, **22**, 1120–45.

Garsten, C. (1999). 'Betwixt and between: temporary employees as liminal subjects in temporary organisations'. *Organisation Studies*, **20**(4), 601–17.

Gayá Wicks, P. and A. Rippin (2010). 'Art as experience: an inquiry into art and leadership using dolls and doll-making'. *Leadership*, **6**, 259–78.

Geertz, C. (1975). *The Interpretation of Cultures.* London: Hutchinson.

Geertz, C. (1983). *Local Knowledge: Further Essays in Interpretive Anthropology.* New York: Basic Books.

Gellner, E. (1964). *Thought and Change.* London: Weidenfeld and Nicolson.

George, B. (2003). *Authentic Leadership: Rediscovering the Secrets of Creating Lasting Value.* San Francisco, CA: Jossey-Bass.

Gergen, K.J. (2009). *Realities and Relationships: Soundings in Social Construction.* Boston, MA: Harvard University Press.

Gerth, H. and C. Wright Mills (1954). *Character and Social Structure.* London: Routledge.

Gibb, C.A. (1954). 'Leadership'. In G. Lindzey and E. Aronson (eds), *The Handbook of Social Psychology*, Vol. 4, second edn. Reading, MA: Addison-Wesley, pp. 205–83.

Goffee, R. and G. Jones (2000). 'Why should anyone be led by you?', *Harvard Business Review*, September–October, 63–70.

Goodenow, C. (1993). 'Classroom belonging among early adolescent students: relationships to motivation and achievement'. *Journal of Early Adolescence*, **13**, 21–43.

Goodenow, C. and K. Grady (1993). 'The relationship of school belonging and friends' values to academic motivation among urban adolescent students'. *Journal of Experimental Education*, **62**, 60–71.

Gosling, J., R. Bolden and G. Petrov (2009). 'Distributed leadership in higher education: what does it accomplish?', *Leadership*, **5**, 299–310.

Graen, G.B. and M. Uhl-Bien (1995). 'A relationship-based approach to leadership: development of a leader-member exchange (LMX) theory of leadership over 25 years: applying a multilevel multidomain perspective'. *Leadership Quarterly*, **6**, 219–47.

Greenleaf, R.K. (1977). *Servant Leadership: A Journey into the Nature of Legitimate Power and Greatness.* Mahwah, NJ: Paulist Press.

Griffey, E. and B. Jackson (2010). 'The portrait as leader: commissioned portraits and the power of tradition'. *Leadership*, **6**(2), 133–57.

Grint. K. (2005a). 'Problems, problems, problems: the social construction of leadership'. *Human Relations*, **58**, 1467–94.

Grint, K. (2005b). *Leadership: Limits and Possibilities.* London: Palgrave Macmillan.

Grint, K. (2010a). 'Leadership: an enemy of the people?', *International Journal of Leadership in the Public Services*, **6**(4), 22–25.

Grint, K. (2010b). 'The sacred in leadership: separation, sacrifice and silence'. *Organizations Studies,* **31**(1), 89–107.

Grint, K. and B. Jackson (2010). 'Toward "socially constructive" social constructions of leadership'. *Management Communication Quarterly*, **24**(2), 238–355.

Gronn, P. (2002). 'Distributed leadership as a unit of analysis'. *Leadership Quarterly*, **13**, 423–51.

Gronn, P. (2008). 'The future of distributed leadership'. *Journal of Educational Administration*, **46**, 141–58.

Gronn, P. (2009a). 'Leadership configurations'. *Leadership*, **5**, 381–94.

Gronn, P. (2009b). 'Hybrid leadership'. In K. Leithwood, B. Mascall and T. Strauss (eds), *Distributed Leadership According to the Evidence*. New York: Routledge, pp. 17–40.

Guillet de Monthoux, P., C. Gustafsson and S.E. Sjöstrand (2007). *Aesthetic Leadership: Managing Fields of Flow in Art and Business*. London: Palgrave Macmillan.

Gusfield, J.R. (1975). *Community: A Critical Response*. New York: Harper & Row.

Habermas, J. (1984). *The Theory of Communicative Action, Volume 1: Reason and Rationalisation in Society*. London: Heinemann.

Hall, S. and T. Jefferson (eds) (1976). *Resistance through Rituals*. London: Hutchinson.

Hansen, H. and R. Bathhurst (2011). 'Aesthetics and leadership'. In A. Bryman, D. Collinson, K. Grint, B. Jackson and M. Uhl-Bien (eds), *The Sage Handbook of Leadership*. London: Sage, pp. 255–66.

Hansen, H., A. Ropo and E. Sauer (2007). 'Aesthetic leadership'. *Leadership Quarterly*, **18**, 544–60.

Harding, N., H. Lee, J. Ford and M. Learmonth (2011). 'Leadership and charisma: a desire that cannot speak its name?', *Human Relations*, **64**(7), 927–49.

Harris, A. (2004). 'Distributed leadership: leading or misleading'. *Educational Management and Administration*, **32**, 11–24.

Harris, A. (2008). *Distributed School Leadership: Developing Tomorrow's Leaders*. London: Routledge.

Harris, A. (2009a). 'Distributed leadership and knowledge creation'. In K. Leithwood, B. Mascall and T. Strauss (eds), *Distributed Leadership According to the Evidence*. New York: Routledge, pp. 253–66.

Harris, A. (ed.) (2009b). *Distributed Leadership: Different Perspectives*. London: Routledge.

Harter, N. (2006). *Clearings in the Forest: On the Study of Leadership*. West Lafayette, IN: Purdue University Press.

Hatch, M.J., M. Kostera and A.J. Kozminski (2005). *The Three Faces of Leadership: Manager, Artist, Priest.* Malden, MA: Blackwell.

Hawkins, B. and G.P. Edwards (forthcoming). 'Liminality and threshold concepts and leadership learning: an initial exploration'. *Management Learning.* Expected publication April 2015, available on onlinefirst at http://mlq.sagepub.com/content/early/recent until that date.

Hebdige, D. (1979). *Subculture: The Meaning of Style.* London: Methuen.

Hill, N.C. and J.B. Ritchie (1977). 'The effect of self-esteem on leadership: a paradigm and a review'. *Group and Organization Management*, **2**(4), 491–503.

Hollander, E.P. (1995). 'Ethical challenges in the leader-follower relationship'. *Business Ethics Quarterly*, **5**(1), 55–65.

Hollander, E.P. and J.W. Julian (1969). 'Contemporary trends in the analysis of leadership processes'. *Psychological Bulletin*, **71**(5), 387–97.

Hosking, D.M. (1988). 'Organising, leadership and skilful process'. *Journal of Management Studies*, **25**, 147–66.

Hosking, D.M. (2007). 'Not leaders, not followers: a post-modern discourse of leadership processes'. In B. Shamir, R. Pillai, M. Bligh and M. Uhl-Bien (eds), *Follower-centered Perspectives on Leadership: A Tribute to the Memory of James R. Meindl.* Greenwich, CT: Information Age Publishing, pp. 243–63.

House, R.J. (1977). 'A 1976 theory of charismatic leadership'. In J.G. Hunt and L.L Larson (eds), *Leadership: The Cutting Edge.* Carbondale, IL: Southern Illinois University Press., pp. 189–207.

House, R.J., P.J. Hanges, M. Javidan, P.W. Dorfman and V. Gupta (eds) (2004). *Culture, Leadership, and Organizations: The GLOBE Study of 62 Societies.* Thousand Oaks, CA: Sage.

Howard, V.A. (1996). 'The aesthetic face of leadership'. *Journal of Aesthetic Education*, **30**(4), 21–37.

Isaacs, T. (2011). *Moral Responsibility in Collective Contexts.* Oxford: Oxford University Press.

Jackson, B. and K. Parry (2008). *A Very Short, Fairly Interesting and Reasonably Cheap Book About Studying Leadership.* London: Sage.

Jacobs, R.L. and D.C. McClelland (1994). 'Moving up the corporate ladder: a longitudinal study of the leadership motive pattern and managerial success in women and men'. *Consulting Psychology Journal: Practice and Research*, **46**(1), 32–41.

Jepson, D. (2009). 'Leadership context: the importance of departments'. *Leadership and Organisation Development Journal*, **30**, 36–52.

Jones, A. (2005). 'The anthropology of leadership: culture and corporate leadership in the American South'. *Leadership*, **1**, 259–78.

Kamau, L.J. (2002). 'Liminality, communitas, charisma and community'. In S. Love Brown (ed.), *Intentional Community: An Anthropological Perspective*. New York: State University of New York Press, pp. 17–40.

Kant, I. (1790). *Critique of Judgement*. Berlin.

Kanter, R.M. (1972). *Commitment and Community: Communes and Utopias in Sociological Perspective*. Cambridge, MA: Harvard Business School Press.

Kellerman, B. (2004). *Bad Leadership: What It Is, How It Happens, Why It Matters*. Boston, MA: Harvard Business School Press.

Kelly, S. (2014). 'Towards a negative ontology of leadership'. *Human Relations*, **67**, 923–46.

Kempster, S. and J. Stewart (2010). 'Becoming a leader: a co-produced autoethnographic exploration of situated learning of leadership practice'. *Management Learning*, **41**(2), 205–19.

Kerr, S. and J.M. Jermier (1978). 'Substitutes for leadership: their meaning and measurement'. *Organizational Behavior and Human Performance*, **22**(3), 375–403.

Klima, I. (1999). *Between Security and Insecurity*, translated by G. Turner. London: Thames and Hudson.

Knights, D. and M. O'Leary (2005). 'Reflecting on corporate scandals: the failure of ethical leadership'. *Business Ethics: A European Review*, **14**(4), 359–66.

Knights, D. and M. O'Leary (2006). 'Leadership, ethics and responsibility to the other'. *Journal of Business Ethics*, **67**, 125–37.

Kotter, J.P. (1990). *A Force for Change: How Leadership Differs From Management*. New York: The Free Press.

Krantz, J. (2006). 'Leadership, betrayal and adaption'. *Human Relations*, **59**(2), 221–40.

Ladkin, D. (2006). 'The enchantment of the charismatic leader: charisma reconsidered as aesthetic encounter'. *Leadership*, **2**, 165–79.

Ladkin, D. (2008). 'Leading beautifully: how mastery, congruence and purpose create the aesthetic of embodied leadership practice'. *Leadership Quarterly*, **19**(1), 31–41.

Ladkin, D. and S. Taylor (2010). 'Leadership as art: variations on a theme'. *Leadership*, **6**, 235–41.

Larsson, M. and S.E. Lundholm (2010). 'Leadership as work-embedded influence: a micro-discursive analysis of an everyday interaction in a bank'. *Leadership*, **6**(2), 159–84.

Lasch, C. (1979). *The Culture of Narcissism*, Warner edn. New York: Norton and Co.

Lash, S. (1994). 'Reflexivity and its doubles: structures, aesthetics, community'. In U. Beck, A. Giddens and S. Lash (eds), *Reflexive Modernisation: Politics, Tradition and Aesthetics in the Modern Social Order.* Cambridge: Polity Press, pp. 110–73.

Leach, E.R. (1954). *Political Systems of Highland Burma.* London: G. Bell & Son.

Leach, N. (2002). 'Belonging: towards a theory of identification with space'. In J. Hillier and E. Rooksby (eds), *Habitus: A Sense of Place.* Aldershot: Ashgate, pp. 281–95.

Learmonth, M. (2005). 'Doing things with words: the case of "management" and "administration"'. *Public Administration*, **83**(3), 617–37.

Lee. L. (1959). *Cider with Rosie.* London: Random House.

Leithwood, K., B. Mascall and T. Strauss (2009). *Distributed Leadership According to the Evidence.* New York: Routledge.

Levay, C. (2010). 'Charismatic leadership in resistance to change'. *Leadership Quarterly*, **21**, 127–43.

Lewis, C.S. (1961). *The Four Loves.* New York: Harcourt Brace and Company.

Lichterman, P. (1996). *The Search for Political Community.* Cambridge: Cambridge University Press.

Lipman-Blumen, J. (2005). *The Allure of Toxic Leaders.* Oxford: Oxford University Press.

Little, G. (1993). *Friendship: Being Ourselves with Others.* Carlton North, VIC: Scribe Publications.

Lord, R.G. and C.G. Emrich (2001). 'Thinking outside the box by looking inside the box: extending the cognitive revolution in leadership research'. *Leadership Quarterly*, **11**, 551–79.

Love Brown, S. (2002). 'Introduction'. In S. Love Brown (ed.),

Intentional Community: An Anthropological Perspective. New York: State University of New York Press, pp. 1–16.

Low, S.M. and D. Lawrence-Zúñiga (eds) (2003). *The Anthropology of Space and Place: Locating Culture.* Malden, MA: Blackwell.

Luthans, F. and B.J. Avolio (2003). 'Authentic leadership: a positive developmental approach'. In K.S. Cameron, J.E. Dutton and R.E. Quinn (eds), *Positive Organizational Scholarship.* San Francisco, CA: Barrett-Koehler, pp. 241–61.

Ma, X. (2003). 'Sense of belonging to school: can schools make a difference?'. *Journal of Educational Research*, **96**(6), 340–9.

Mabey, C. and T. Freeman (2011). 'Reflections on leadership and place'. In C. Collinge, J. Gibney and C. Mabey (eds), *Leadership and Place.* New York: Routledge, pp. 139–56.

MacIntyre, A. (1984). *After Virtue.* London and Notre Dame: Duckworth and University of Notre Dame Press, reprinted in 1991.

MacMurray, J. (1996). *The Personal World.* Edinburgh: Floris Books.

Maffesoli, M. (1996). *The Time of Tribes: The Decline of Individualism in Mass Society.* London: Sage.

Maine, H. (1871). *Village Communities of the East and West*, London: John Murray.

Manz, C.C. and H.P. Sims (1980). 'Self management as a substitute for leadership: a social learning theory perspective'. *Academy of Management Review*, **5**(3), 361–7.

Marx, K. and F. Engels (1848). *The Communist Manifesto.* London: The Educational Society.

Marx, K. (1970). *A Contribution to the Critique of Political Economy*, translated by Ryazanskaya, Maurice Dobb (ed.). London: Lawrence and Wishart.

Maslow, A. (1962). *Towards a Psychology of Belonging.* Princeton, NJ: Van Nostrand.

Massey, D. (1993). 'Power geometrics and a progressive sense of place'. In J. Bird, B. Curtis, T. Putnam, G. Robertson and L. Tickner (eds), *Mapping the Futures: Local Cultures, Global Changes.* London: Routledge.

Massey, D. (2005). *For Space.* London: Sage.

May, V. (2011). 'Self, belonging and social change'. *Sociology*, **45**, 363–78.

McGregor, D. (1966). *Leadership and Motivation.* Cambridge, MA: MIT Press.

McMillan, D. and D.M. Chavis (1986). 'Sense of community: a definition and a theory'. *Journal of Community Psychology*, **14**, 6–23.

Mead, G. (2014). *Telling the Story: The Heart and Soul of Successful Leadership.* San Francisco, CA: Jossey-Bass.

Meindl, J. (1995). 'The romance of leadership as a follower-centric theory: a social constructionist approach'. *Leadership Quarterly*, **6**(3), 329–41.

Meindl, J., S.B. Ehrlich and J.M. Dukerich (1985). 'The romance of leadership'. *Administrative Science Quarterly*, **30**(1), 78–102.

Mendonca, M. and R. Kanungo (2007). *Ethical Leadership.* New York: Open University Press and McGraw Hill.

Miller, L. (2003). 'Belonging to country: a philosophical anthropology'. *Journal of Australian Studies*, **27**, 215–23.

Mintzberg, H. (2004). *Managers Not MBAs: A Hard Look at the Soft Practice of Managing and Management Development.* San Francisco, CA: Berrett-Koehler.

Mintzberg, H. and J. Gosling (2003). 'The five minds of a manager'. *Harvard Business Review*, November, 54–63.

Moore, G.E. (1902). *Principa Ethica.* Cambridge: Cambridge University Press.

Nancy, J.-L. (1991). *The Inoperative Community.* Minneapolis, MN: University of Minnesota Press.

Nel, D., L. Pitt. and R. Watson (1989). 'Business ethics: defining the twilight zone'. *Journal of Business Ethics*, **8**, 781–91.

Nietzsche, F. (1974). *The Gay Science*, translated by W. Kaufman. London: Random House.

Norris, S. (2001). 'Been there, done that: networking'. *The Times,* p. 8.

Osborn, R.N. and R. Marion (2009). 'Contextual leadership, transformational leadership and the performance of international innovation seeking alliances'. *Leadership Quarterly*, **20**, 191–206.

Osborn, R.N., J.G. Hunt and L.R. Jauch (2002). 'Toward a contextual theory of leadership'. *Leadership Quarterly*, **13**(6), 797–837.

Palmer, P. (2000). *Let Your Lie Speak: Listening for the Inner Voice of Vocation.* San Francisco, CA: Jossey-Bass.

Peteet, J. (1995). 'Transforming trust: dispossession and empowerment among Palestinian refugees'. In E. Valentine Daniel and J.C. Knudsen (eds), *Mistrusting Refugees.* Berkeley, CA: University of California Press, pp. 168–86..

Phal, R. (2000). *On Friendship.* Cambridge: Polity Press.

Pocock, J.G.A. (1973). *Politics, Language and Time: Essays on Political Thought and History.* New York: Atheneum.

Porter, L.W. and G.B. McLaughlin (2006). 'Leadership and the organizational context: like the weather?', *Leadership Quarterly,* **17**, 559–76.

Pullen, A. and S. Vachhani (2013). 'The materiality of leadership'. *Leadership,* **9**(3), 315–19.

Pye, A. (2005). 'Leadership and organising: sense-making in action'. *Leadership,* **7**, 31–49.

Renan, E. (1984). *Marc Aurèle.* Paris: Livre de Poche.

Renfro-Sargent, M. (2002). 'The borderlands of community: refugee camps, intentional communities and liminality'. In S. Love Brown (ed.), *Intentional Community: An Anthropological Perspective.* New York: State University of New York Press, pp. 83–106.

Resick, C.J., G.S. Martin, M.A. Keating, M.W. Dickson, H.K. Kwan and C. Peng (2011). 'What ethical leadership means to me: Asian, American and European perspectives'. *Journal of Business Ethics,* **101**, 435–57.

Ricoeur, P. (1992). *Oneself as Another,* translated by K. Blamey. Chicago, IL: University of Chicago Press.

Rieff, P. (1966). *The Triumph of the Therapeutic: The Uses of Faith After Freud.* London: Chatto and Windus.

Riggio R.E., I. Chaleff and J. Lipman-Blumen (2008). *The Art of Followership: How Great Followers Create Great Leaders and Organizations.* San Francisco, CA: Jossey-Bass.

Roeser, R.W., C. Midgley and T.C. Urdan (1996). 'Perceptions of the school psychological environment and early adolescents' psychological and behavioural functioning in school: the mediating role of goals and belonging'. *Journal of Educational Psychology,* **88**(3), 408–22.

Ropo, A. and J. Parviainen (2001). 'Leadership and bodily knowledge in expert organizations: epistemological rethinking'. *Scandanavian Journal of Management,* **17**(1), 1–18.

Ropo, A. and E. Sauer (2008). 'Dances of leadership: bridging theory and practice through an aesthetic approach'. *Journal of Management and Organization,* **14**(5), 560–72.

Ropo, A., J. Parviainen.and N. Koivunen (2002). 'Aesthetics in leadership: from absent bodies to social bodily presence'. In K.W. Parry and J.R. Meindl (eds), *Grounding Leadership Theory and*

Research: Issues and Perspectives. Greenwich, CT: Information Age Publishing, pp. 21–38.

Rosenblum, N. (1987). *Another Liberalism: Romanticism and the Reconstruction of Liberal Thought.* Cambridge, MA: Harvard University Press.

Sandal, M. (1982). *Liberalism and the Limits of Justice.* Cambridge: Cambridge University Press.

Saskin, M. (1988). 'The visionary leader'. In J.A. Conger and R.A. Kanungo (eds), *Charismatic Leadership: The Elusive Factor in Organizational Effectiveness.* San Francisco, CA: Jossey-Bass, pp. 122–60.

Saussure, F. (1966). *Course in General Linguistics.* New York: McGraw-Hill.

Savage, M., G. Bagnall and B. Longhurst (2005). *Globalization and Belonging: The Suburbanization of Identity.* London: Sage.

Schaar, J. (1983). 'The question of justice'. *Raritan*, **3**, 107–29.

Schedlitzki, D. and G.P. Edwards (2014). *Studying Leadership: Traditional and Critical Approaches.* London: Sage.

Schein, E.H. (2004). *Organisational Culture*, 3rd edn. San Francisco, CA: Jossey-Bass.

Schyns, B., A. Tymon, T. Kiefer and R. Kerschreiter (2013). 'New ways to leadership development: a picture paints a thousand words'. *Management Learning*, **44**(1), 11–24.

Sennett, R. (1998). *The Corrosion of Character.* New York: Norton.

Sennett, R. (1999). 'Growth and failure: the new political economy and its culture'. In M. Featherstone and S. Lash (eds), *Spaces of Culture: City-Nation-World.* London: Sage, pp. 14–26.

Shamir, B. and G. Eilam (2005). 'What's your story: a life stories approach to authentic leadership development'. *Leadership Quarterly*, **16**(3), 395–417.

Shamir, B., R. Pillai, M.C. Bligh and M. Uhl-Bien (eds) (2007). *Follower-centred Perspectives on Leadership: A Tribute to the Memory of James R. Meindl.* Charlotte, NC: Information Age Press, pp. 5–7.

Shields, R. (1996). 'Foreword: masses or tribes?'. In M. Maffesoli (ed.), *The Time of Tribes.* London: Sage, pp. ix–xi.

Shotter, J. (1993). *Cultural Politics of Everyday Life.* Buckingham: Open University Press.

Simpson, R., J. Sturges and P. Weight (2010). 'Transient, unsettling and creative space: experiences of liminality through the accounts of Chinese students on a UK-based MBA'. *Management Learning*, **41**(1), 53–70.

Sinclair, A. (2005). 'Body and management pedagogy'. *Gender, Work and Organization*, **12**(1), 89–104.

Smircich, L. and G. Morgan (1982). 'Leadership: the management of meaning'. *Journal of Applied Behavioural Science*, **18**(3), 257–73.

Sparrowe, R. and R.C. Liden (1997). 'Process and structure in leader-member exchange'. *Academy of Management Review*, **22**, 522–52.

Sparrowe, R. and R.C. Liden (2005). 'Two routes to influence: integrating leader-member exchange and network perspectives'. *Administrative Science Quarterly*, **50**(4), 505–35.

Spencer, H. (1858). *Progress: Its Law and Causes.* London: Longman, Brown, Green, Longmans and Roberts.

Spillane, J.P. (2006). *Distributed Leadership.* San Francisco, CA: Jossey-Bass.

Spillane, J.P. and J.B. Diamond (2007). *Distributed Leadership in Practice.* New York: Teachers College Press.

Springborg, C. (2010). 'Leadership as art – leaders coming to their senses'. *Leadership*, **6**, 243–58.

Stern-Gillet, S. (1995). *Aristotle's Philosophy of Friendship.* Albany, NY: State University of New York Press.

Sturdy, A., M. Schwarz and A. Spicer (2006). 'Guess who's coming to dinner? Structures and uses of liminality in strategic management consultancy'. *Human Relations*, **59**(7), 929–60.

Sullivan, L.E. (1988). *Icanchu's Drum: An orientation to Meaning in the History of Anthropology.* New York: The Free Press.

Sutherland, I. (2013). 'Arts-based methods in leadership development: affording aesthetic workspaces, reflexivity and memories with momentum'. *Management Learning*, **44**(1), 25–43.

Sutherland, I. and A. Walravens (eds) (2011). *Artful Leadership: Reflections from Executive MBA Participants.* Bled, Slovenia: Bled School of Management.

Sveiby, K. (2011). 'Collective leadership with power symmetry: lessons from Aboriginal prehistory'. *Leadership*, **7**(4), 385–414.

Taylor, C. (1989). *Sources of Self.* Cambridge: Cambridge University Press.

Taylor, M. (1982). *Community, Anarchy and Liberty.* Cambridge: Cambridge University Press.

Tempest, S. and K. Starkey (2004). 'The effects of liminality on individual and organisational learning'. *Organisation Studies*, **25**(4), 507–27.

Thornborrow, T. and A.D. Brown (2009). 'Being regimented: aspiration, discipline and identity work in the British Parachute Regiment'. *Organisation Studies*, **30**(4), 355–76.

Thorpe, R., J. Gold and J. Lawler (2011). 'Locating distributed leadership'. *International Journal of Management Reviews*, **13**(3), 239–50.

Thurston, P.W. and R.T. Clift (1996). *Distributed Leadership: School Improvement through Collaboration*. Greenwich, CT: JAI Press.

Tiger, L. (1969). *Men in Groups*. Edinburgh: Thomas Nelson and Sons.

Tilley, C. (1994). *A Phenomenology of Landscape: Places, Paths and Monuments*. Oxford: Berg.

Tourish. D. (2013). *The Dark Side of Transformational Leadership: A Critical Perspective*. London: Routledge.

Tourish, D. (2014). 'Leadership, more or less? A processual, communication perspective on the role of agency in leadership theory'. *Leadership*, **10**, 79–98.

Treviño, L.K., L.P. Hartman and M.E. Brown (2000). 'Moral person and moral manager: how executives develop a reputation for ethical leadership'. *California Management Review*, **42**, 128–42.

Treviño, L.K., M.E. Brown and L.P. Hartman (2003). 'A qualitative investigation of perceived executive ethical leadership: perceptions from inside and outside the executive suite'. *Human Relations*, **55**, 5–37.

Turnbull, S. (2009). '"Worldly" leadership for a global world'. In M. Harvey and J.D. Barbour (eds), *Global Leadership: Portraits of the Past, Visions of the Future*. College Park, MD: International Leadership Association, pp. 82–94.

Turnbull, S., P. Case, G. Edwards, D. Schedlitzki and P. Simpson (2012). *Worldly Leadership*. London: Palgrave Macmillan.

Turner, V.W. (1967). *The Forest of Symbols*. Ithaca, NY: Cornell University Press.

Turner, V.W. (1969). *The Ritual Process: Structure and Anti-structure*. London: Routledge.

Turner, V.W. (1974). *Drama, Fields and Metaphors: Symbolic Action in Human Society*. Ithaca, NY: Cornell University Press.

Turner, V.W. (1979). 'Frame, flow and reflection: ritual and drama in public liminality'. *Japanese Journal of Religious Studies*, **6**(4), 465–99.

Turner, V.W. (1987). 'Betwixt and between: the liminal period in rites of passage'. In L.C. Mahdi, S. Foster and M. Little (eds), *Betwixt and Between: Patterns of Masculine and Feminine Initiation.* Salle, IL: Open Court Publishing, pp. 3–22.

Uhl-Bien, M. (2006). 'Relational leadership theory: exploring the social processes of leadership and organising'. *Leadership Quarterly*, **17**(6), 654–76.

Urban, G. (1996). *Metaphysical Community.* Austin, TX: University of Texas Press.

Van Gennep, A. (1908). *The Rites of Passage*, translated by Solon T. Kimball and Monika B. Vizedom. London: Routledge, reprinted in 1960.

Vernon, M. (2010). *The Meaning of Friendship.* New York: Palgrave Macmillan.

Walumbwa, F.O., B.J. Avolio, W.L. Gardner, T.S. Wernsing and S.J. Peterson (2008). 'Authentic leadership: development and validation of a theory based measure'. *Journal of Management*, **34**(1), 89–126.

Walzer, M. (1983). *Spheres of Justice.* New York: Basic Books.

Warner, L.S. and K. Grint (2006). 'American Indian ways of leading and knowing'. *Leadership*, **2**(2), 225–44.

Weber, M. (1947). *The Theory of Social and Economic Organisations*, translated by T. Parsons. New York: The Free Press.

Weber, M. (1948). 'Politics as vocation'. In H. Gerth and C. Wright Mills (eds), *From Max Weber.* London: Routledge and Kegan Paul, pp. 77–128.

Weber, M. (1949). *Theory of Social and Economic Organisation*, translated by A.M. Henderson and T. Parsons. New York: The Free Press.

Weber, M. (1978). *Economy and Society.* Berkeley, CA: University of California Press.

Weeks, J. (1990). *Coming Out: Homosexual Politics in Britain from the Nineteenth Century to the Present.* London: Quartet Books.

Weir, D. (2012). 'John MacMurray and the philosophical basis of leadership'. Paper presented at EGOS 2012, Helsinski, Finland, 4–7 July.

Wood, M. and D. Ladkin (2008). 'The event's the thing: brief encounters with the leaderful moment'. In K. Turnbull-James and J. Collins (eds), *Leadership Perspectives: Knowledge into Action.* Basingstoke: Palgrave Macmillan, pp. 15–28.

Woodward, J.B. and C. Funk (2010). 'Developing the artist-leader'. *Leadership*, **6**, 295–309.

Yammarino, F.J., S.D. Dionne, C.A. Schriesheim and F. Dansereau (2008). 'Authentic leadership and positive leadership behaviour: a meso, multi-level perspective'. *Leadership Quarterly*, **19**(6), 697–707.

Yip, J. and J.A. Raelin (2012). 'Threshold concepts and modalities for teaching leadership practice'. *Management Learning*, **43**, 333–54.

Young, A.F., A. Russell and J.R. Powers (2004). 'The sense of belonging to a neighbourhood: can it be measured and is it related to health and well being in older women?', *Social Science and Medicine*, **59**, 2627–37.

Yukl, G.A. (2010). *Leadership in Organizations*, 7th edn. Englewood Cliffs, NJ: Prentice-Hall International.

Zoller, H.M. and G.T. Fairhurst (2007). 'Resistance leadership: the overlooked potential in critical organization and leadership studies'. *Human Relations*, **60**(9), 1331–60.

Index